How to Draw THE DARKEST, BADDEST GRAPHIC novels

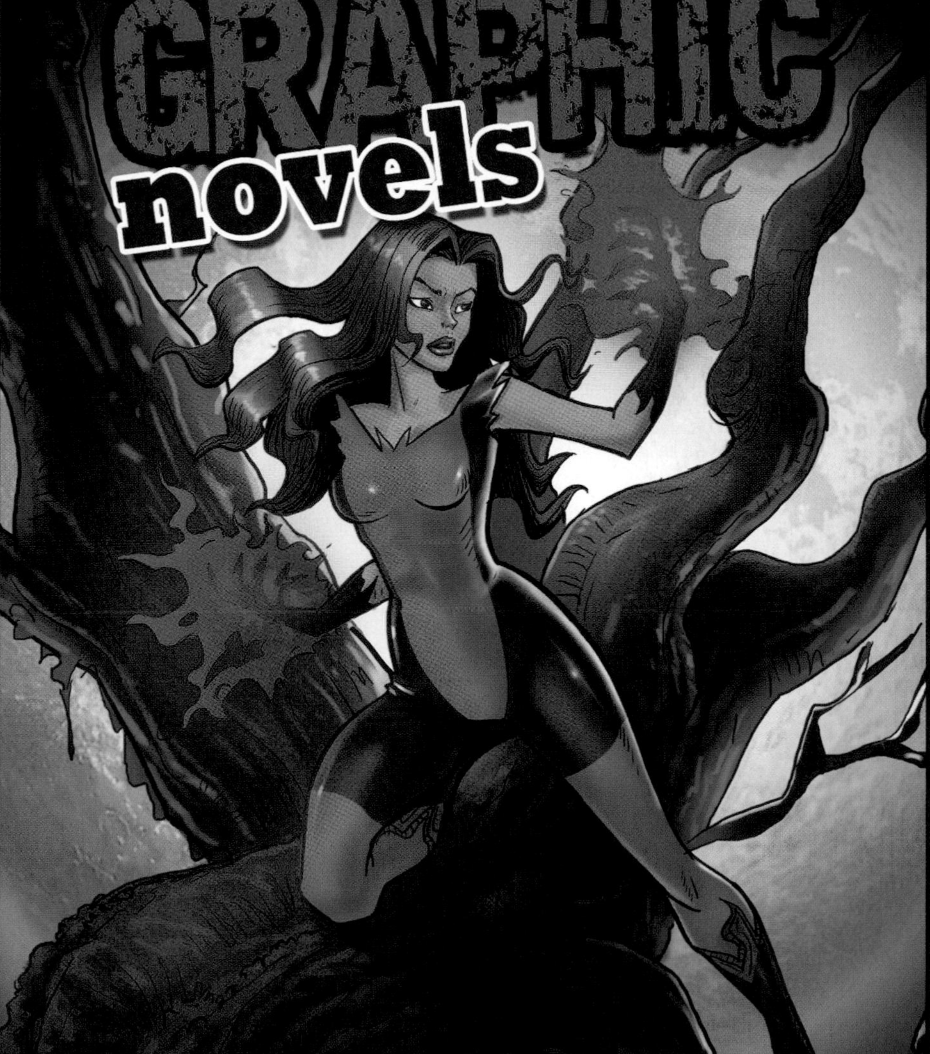

CAPSTONE PRESS
a capstone imprint

Velocity is published by Capstone Press,
151 Good Counsel Drive, P.O. Box 669, Mankato, Minnesota 56002.
www.capstonepub.com

Books published by Capstone Press are manufactured with paper
containing at least 10 percent post-consumer waste.

Library of Congress Cataloging-in-Publication Data
Singh, Asavari.
    How to draw the darkest, baddest graphic novels / by Asavari Singh.
    p. cm. — (Velocity : drawing)
    Includes bibliographical references.
    ISBN 978-1-4296-6594-0 (library binding)
    1. Comic books, strips, etc. — Technique — Juvenile literature. I. Title. II. Series.

NC1764.S563 2012
741.5'1 — dc22   2011010507

Editorial Credits
Author: Asavari Singh
Art Director: Joita Das
Designer: Deepika Verma
Coloring Artists: Aadil Ahmed Siddiqui, Abhijeet Sharma, Danish Zaidi,
                Priyanka Singh, Madhavi Poddar, Vinay Kumar Sharma
Line Artists: Deepak Kumar, Ishan Varma, Martin James, Nishant Mudgal,
                Prithwiraj Samat, Surendra Kumar Tripathi

Printed in the United States of America in Melrose Park, Illinois.
032011
006112LKF11

TABLE of CONTENTS

CHAPTER 1
GRAPHIC NOVELS.................................4

CHAPTER 2
ABOUT FACE....................................6

CHAPTER 3
BODY BASICS 10

CHAPTER 4
STYLE FILE....................................14

CHAPTER 5
SUPERHEROES 16

CHAPTER 6
POWER WOMEN 24

CHAPTER 7
SUPERVILLAINS.................................28

CHAPTER 8
SETTING THE SCENE.............................36

CHAPTER 9
MAKING A STORY...............................42

READ MORE AND
INTERNET SITES...............................48

CHAPTER 1

Graphic Novels

If you can draw and write, and you have a wild imagination, you can make your own graphic novel. Follow the instructions in this book to start your journey.

What are graphic novels?

BLAM! SQUOOSH! CLUNK! If words like these and the pictures on this page look familiar, then you're probably a fan of comic books and graphic novels. Both are stories told through words and pictures. But there's a difference. A comic book usually tells a story in serial form, which means that the story gets published in weekly or monthly installments. A graphic novel tells a full-length story, from start to finish.

Genres

A graphic novel can be about anything! The best-selling genres are superheroes, science fiction, horror, adventure, and crime. Most graphic novels are packed with action and adventure.

Characters

Larger-than-life characters are what make graphic novels work. These could include a superhero on a mission to save mankind, or a supervillain trying to take over the world. More down-to-earth characters include cops on a crusade against crime, and explorers on a quest for great treasure. The central character could even be an ordinary boy or girl thrust into an extraordinary situation or adventure.

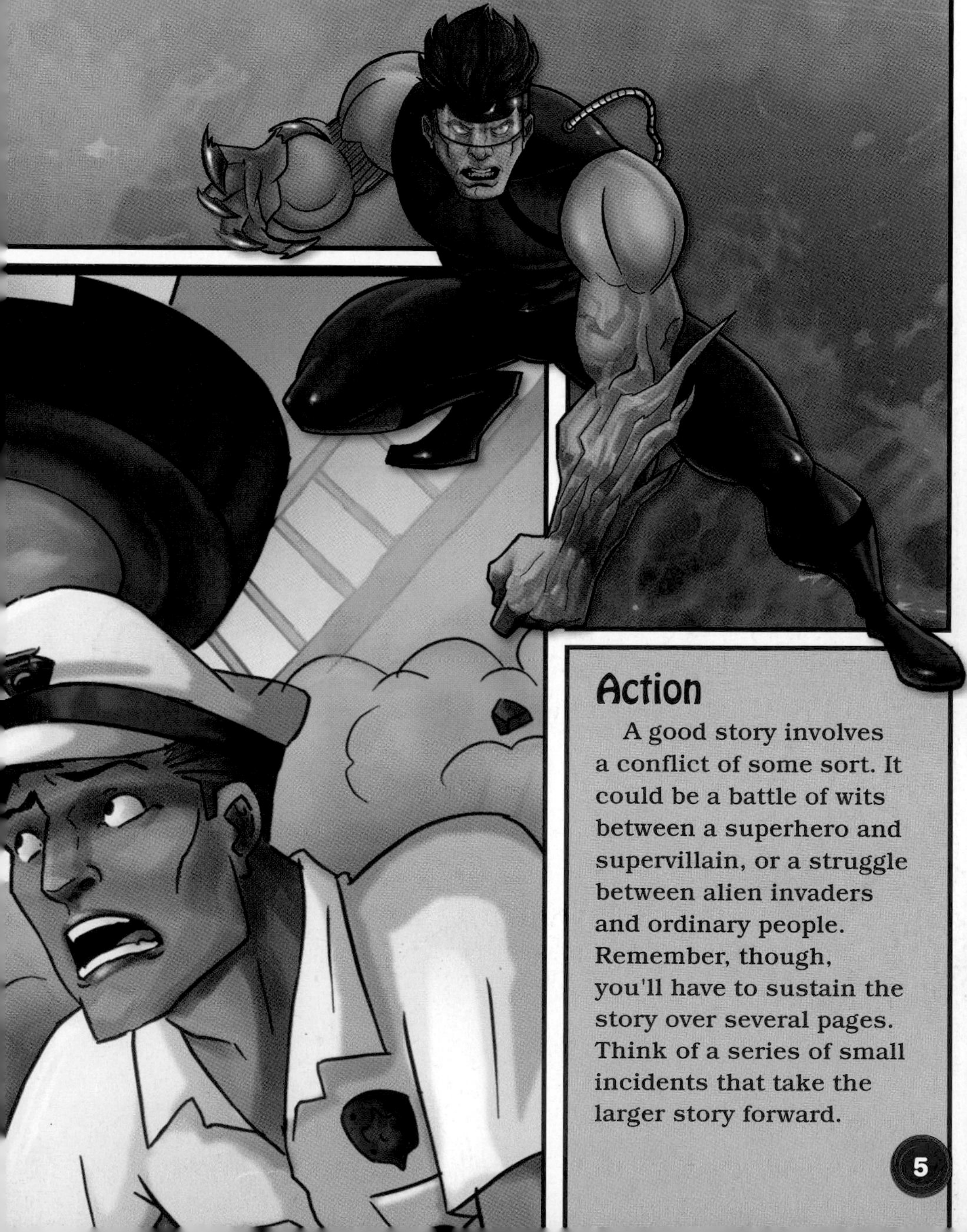

Action

A good story involves a conflict of some sort. It could be a battle of wits between a superhero and supervillain, or a struggle between alien invaders and ordinary people. Remember, though, you'll have to sustain the story over several pages. Think of a series of small incidents that take the larger story forward.

CHAPTER 2

About Face

Learn to make basic male and female faces. Then draw them from different angles and try out new hairstyles.

Basic Faces

For a front view, first draw a circle for the head. Draw lines to divide the face down the middle, as well as across. These guidelines will help you place the features correctly.

Once you make the head, draw straight and slanted lines to shape the cheeks and jaw. Men generally have larger jaws and necks than women.

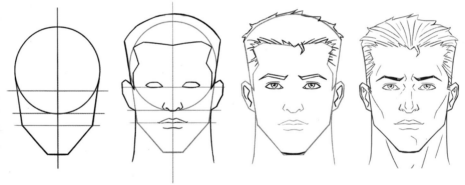

For a face in profile, draw a slightly wider circle. Then make the cheek and jaw as shown. Draw guidelines and place features.

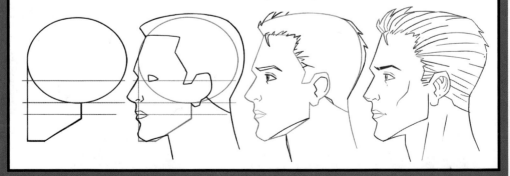

A character's hairstyle can say a lot about his or her personality. Remember to use long strokes of your pencil for a more natural look.

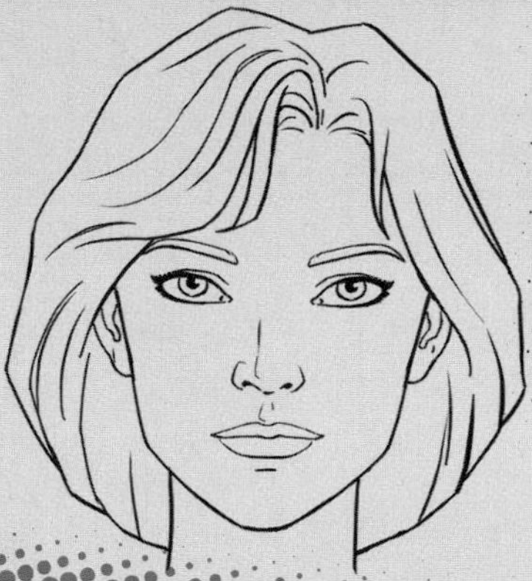

This girl's hair is neither too long nor too short. The bob marks her as an "average Jane", though she could surprise you!

Heroines often have long, flowing tresses. Make the hair wavy and wild to give her a slightly unpredictable look.

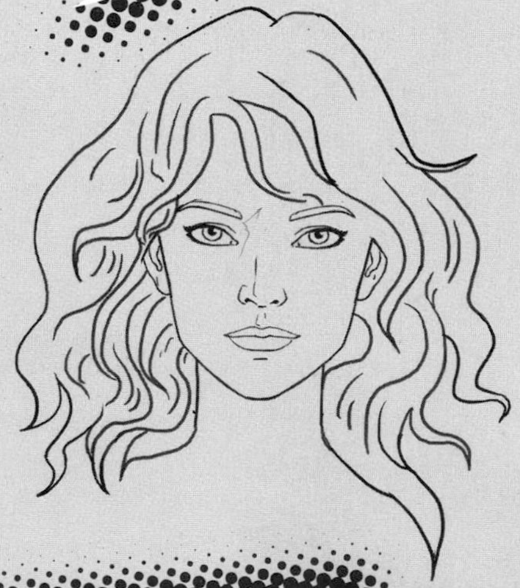

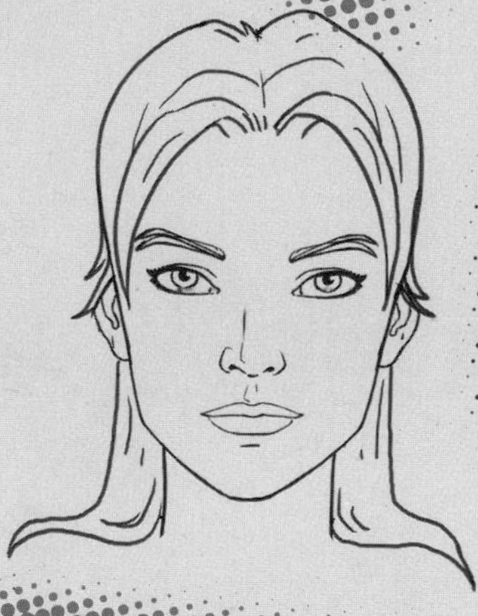

This unusual hairdo makes this character look modern and trendy.

Close, cropped hair with a spiky shape signals a tomboy or rebel.

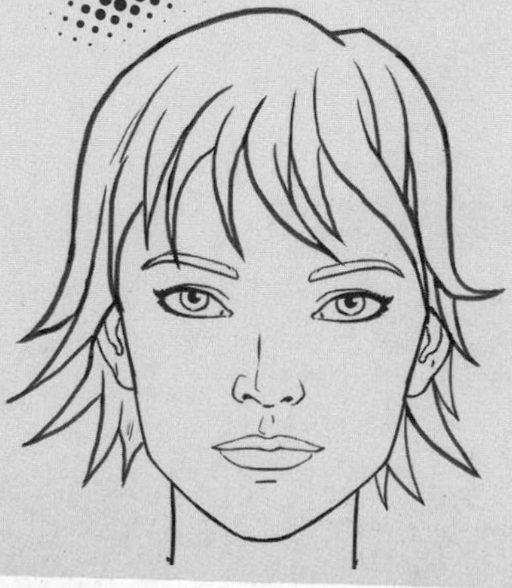

Beyond the Basics

Knowing how to draw a basic face is just the beginning. Everything from the shape of the head to the tilt of an eyebrow is important in creating a character.

Facial Expressions

You don't need to use words to describe a character's age, personality, or feelings. Facial expressions do the trick.

SLY

One eyebrow raised, half smile

SURPRISED

Eyebrows slightly raised, mouth partly open

ANGRY

Big frown, eyes narrowed, lips turned down, teeth showing

HAPPY

Big smile, eyebrows slightly raised. Draw creases at the corners of the mouth.

SCARED

Eyebrows raised, eyes wide, mouth open

DISGUSTED

Slight frown, nose slightly wrinkled, lips turned down

Shape and Size

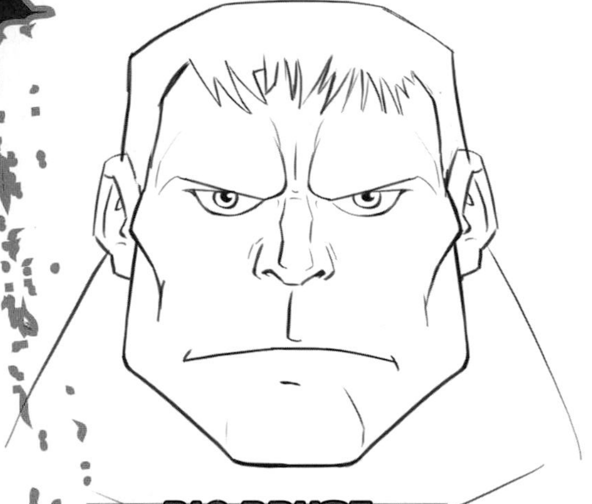

BIG BRUTE

Square head, heavy jaw, short forehead, huge neck

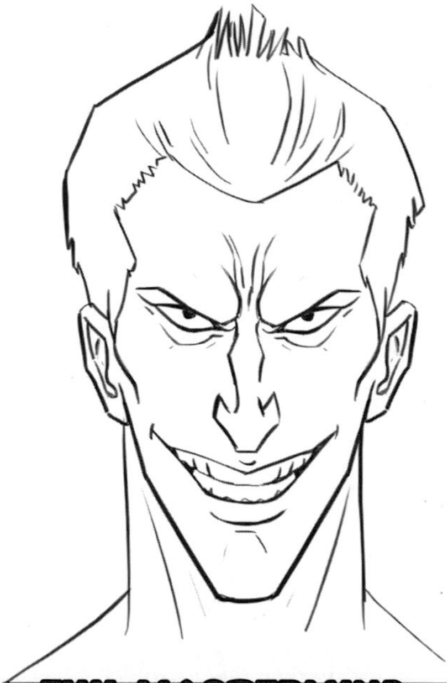

EVIL MASTERMIND

A lean, mean face with narrow eyes; pointed nose and chin

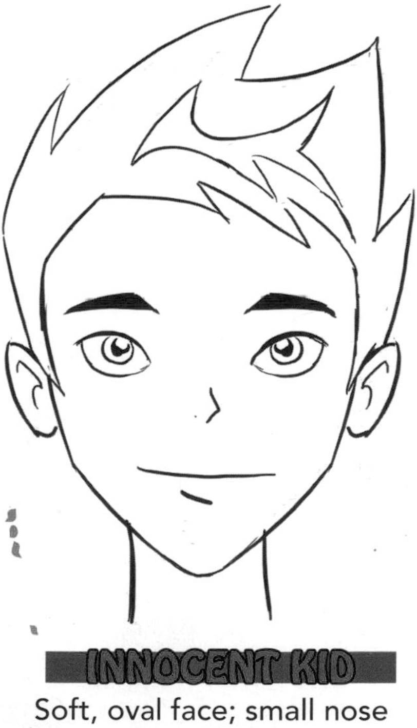

INNOCENT KID

Soft, oval face; small nose and rounded eyes

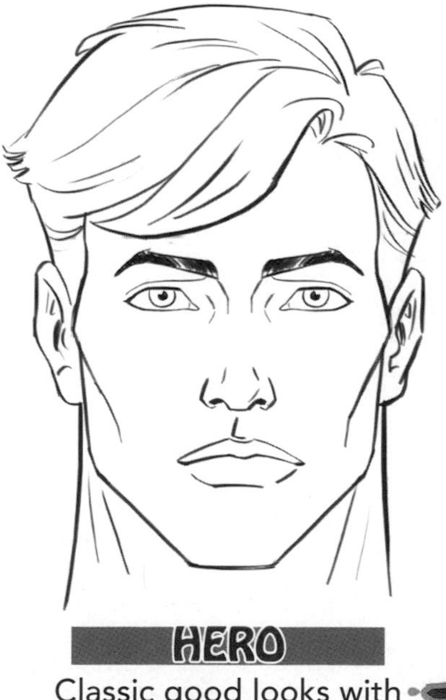

HERO

Classic good looks with a squarish jaw, defined cheekbones, and great hair

CHAPTER 3

BODY BASICS

Practice drawing standard male and female bodies. Once you figure these out, have fun adding muscles and exciting poses.

Bones and Flesh

A stick figure, or wireframe, is the "skeleton" of any character. Males will have broader shoulders, wider waists, and narrower hips than women.

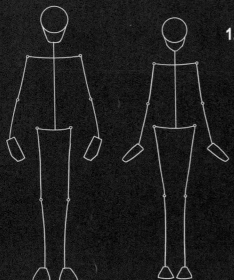

1. Proportions are key to drawing accurate stick figures. The body is equal to roughly eight heads.

Tip

Draw small circles where joints should be. These will help you proportion the limbs correctly. Arms taper off at the elbows and legs at the knees.

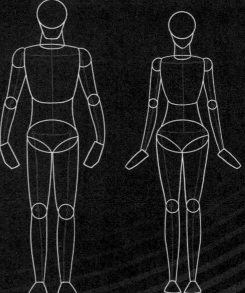

2. Make the joints larger. Add flesh and muscle around the lines and circles. Use solid shapes like spheres, tubes, and curved rectangles for a more 3-D look.

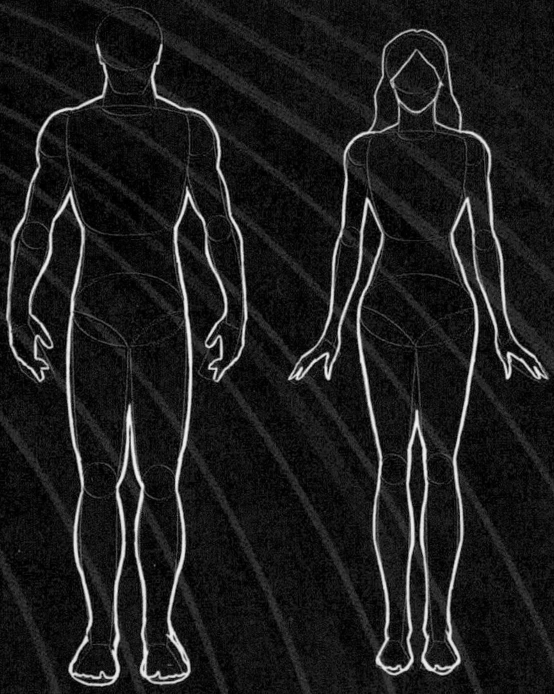

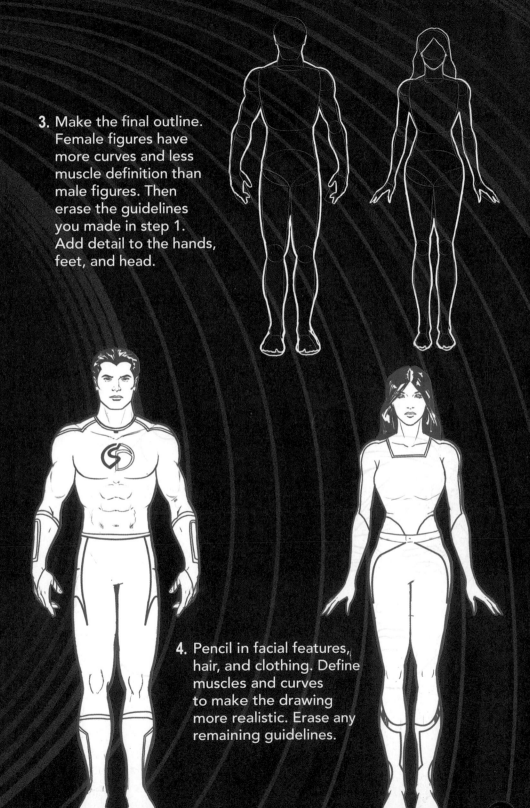

3. Make the final outline. Female figures have more curves and less muscle definition than male figures. Then erase the guidelines you made in step 1. Add detail to the hands, feet, and head.

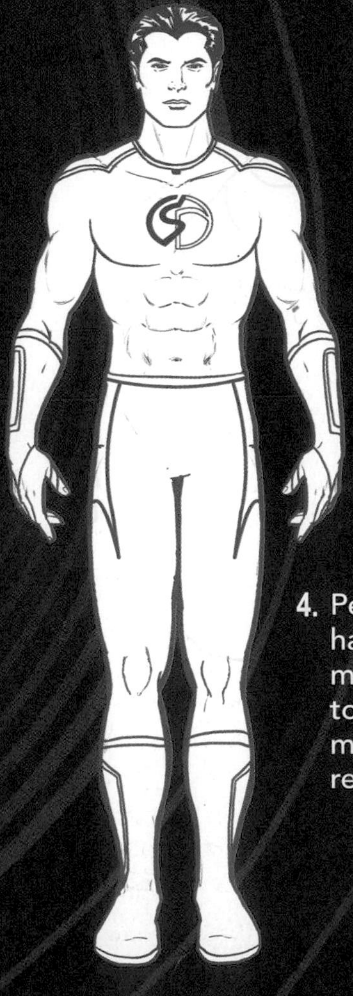

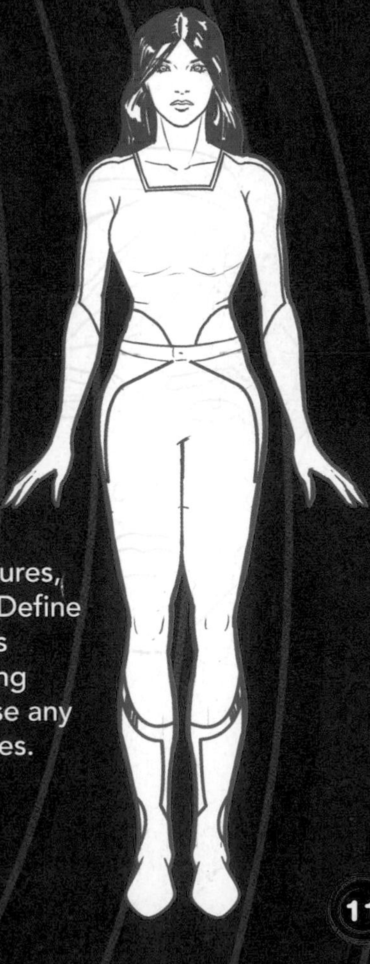

4. Pencil in facial features, hair, and clothing. Define muscles and curves to make the drawing more realistic. Erase any remaining guidelines.

Dynamic Posing

Graphic novels are all about action, so get your characters moving. Practice drawing wireframes in different action positions, and then flesh them out.

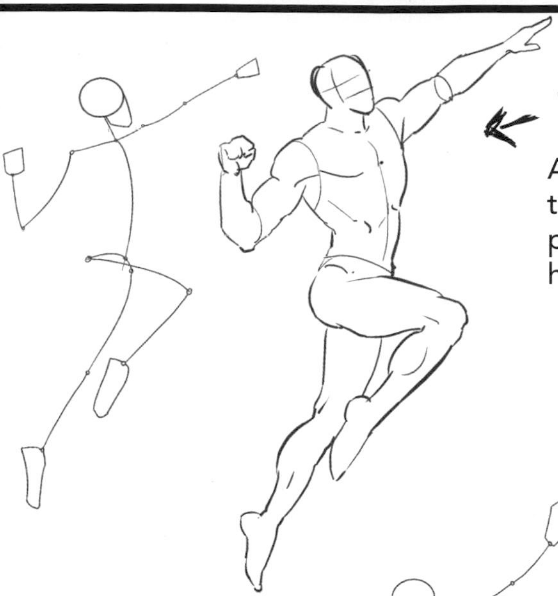

TAKE-OFF

A superhero prepares to fly. Don't forget to pay attention to the hands and feet!

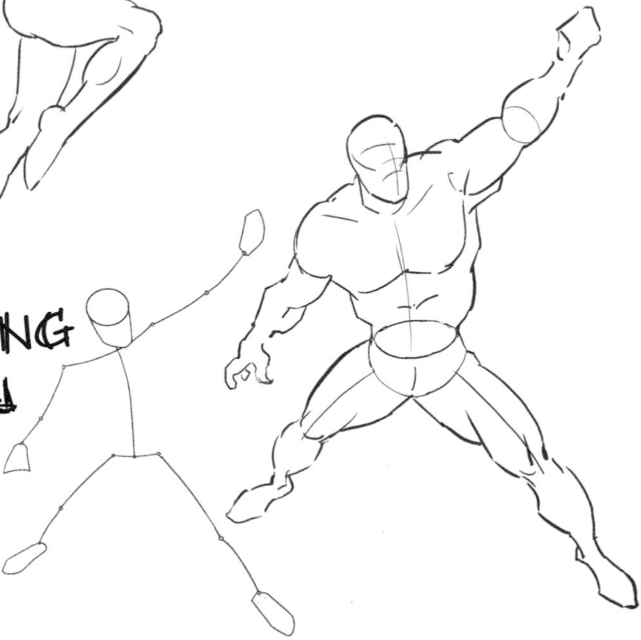

CHALLENGING

This pose says: come get me! The head is facing up, the legs are wide apart, and one hand is closed in an angry fist.

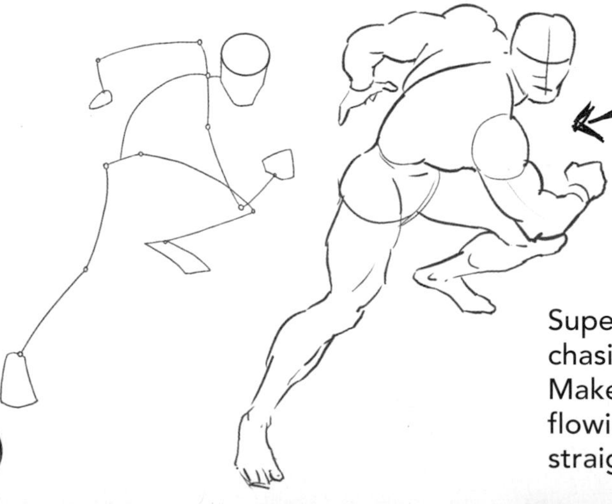

RUNNING

Superheroes are always chasing someone! Make sure you use flowing lines, not stiff, straight ones.

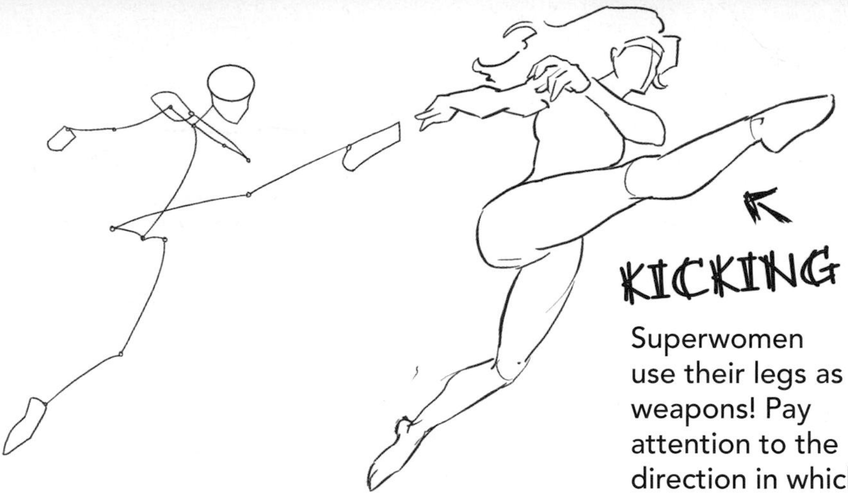

KICKING

Superwomen use their legs as weapons! Pay attention to the direction in which the hair moves. Doing this right makes your drawing more dynamic.

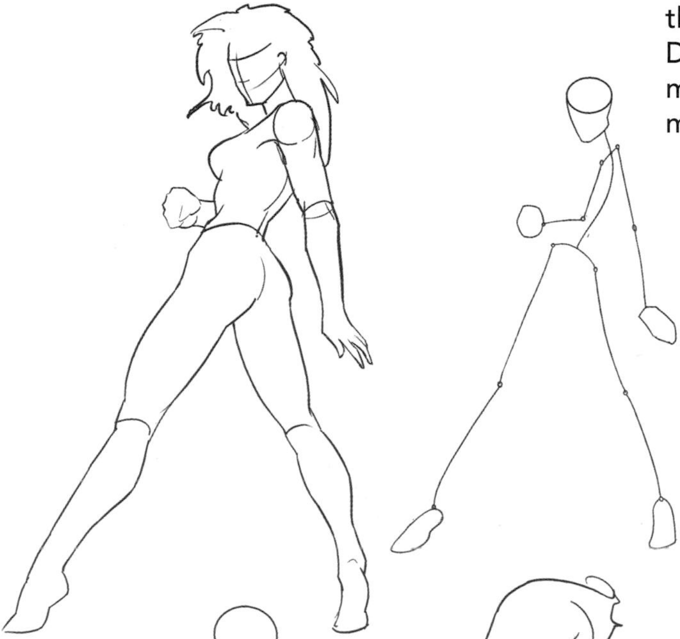

POSING

Superheroines are often drawn in dramatic poses!

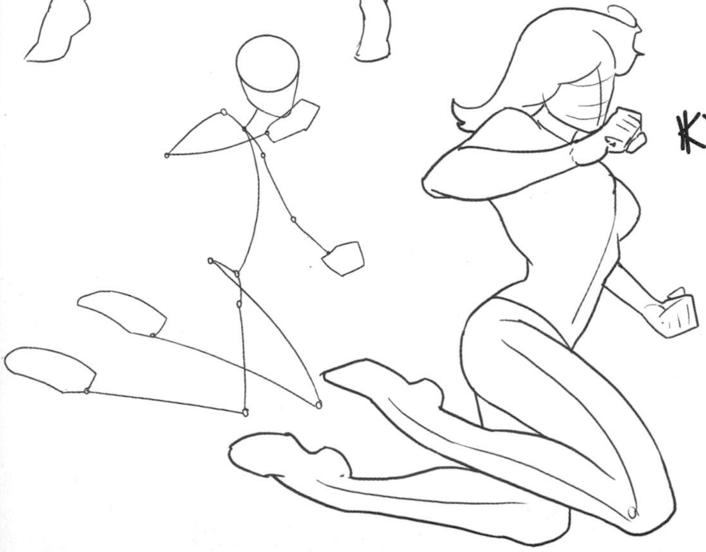

KNEELING

In this posture, one thigh is hidden by the other. Arms are up in a defensive gesture.

CHAPTER 4

STYLE FILE

Clothes and accessories give clues about a character's role, the time period they are from, and how powerful they are.

Dressing up

Superheroes and heroines prefer tight-fitting body suits, big boots, and, sometimes, lethal weapons.

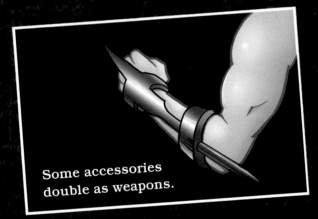

Some accessories double as weapons.

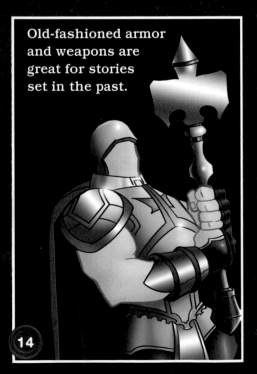

Old-fashioned armor and weapons are great for stories set in the past.

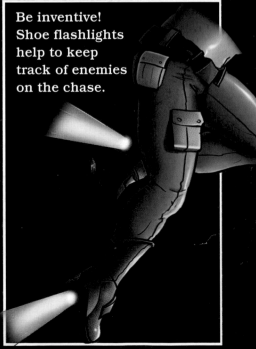

Be inventive! Shoe flashlights help to keep track of enemies on the chase.

Evil characters often dress for maximum damage and minimum detection. Creepy face masks and clawed metal gloves can add instant evil. For a more realistic look, go for dark shades and heavy-duty weapons.

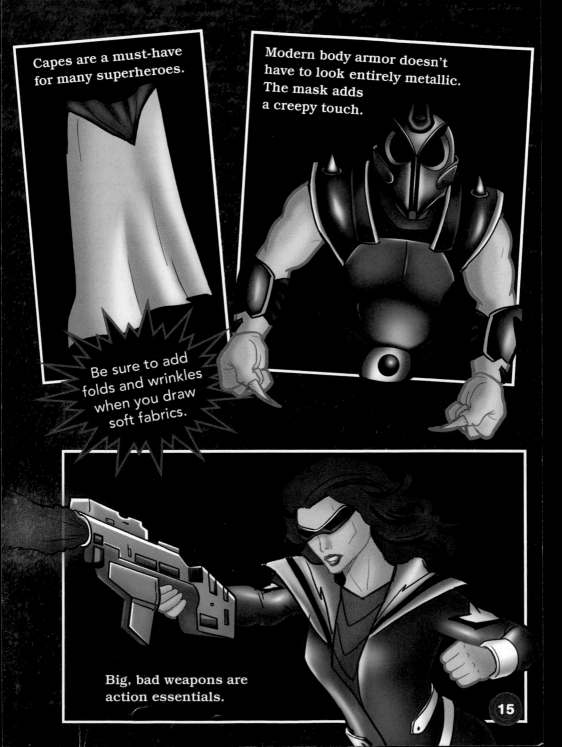

Capes are a must-have for many superheroes.

Modern body armor doesn't have to look entirely metallic. The mask adds a creepy touch.

Be sure to add folds and wrinkles when you draw soft fabrics.

Big, bad weapons are action essentials.

CHAPTER 5

SUPERHEROES

Mighty, muscular, and on a mission, a superhero's main job is to save the world.

Caped Avenger

This superhero is a regular good guy until he puts on his cape. Then he can fly, leap from buildings, and make criminal masterminds very unhappy.

1. Start with a wireframe. Our hero is flying so give the body a streamlined shape, like a bird.

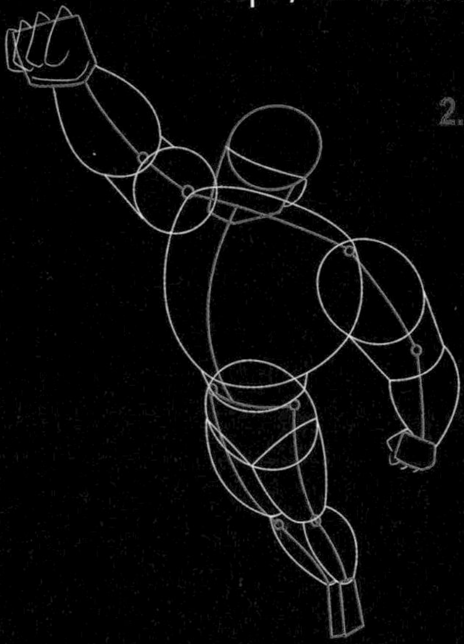

2. Flesh out the wireframe. The torso and arms should be bulky. Make the fist pointing up larger.

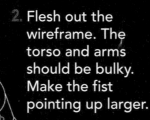

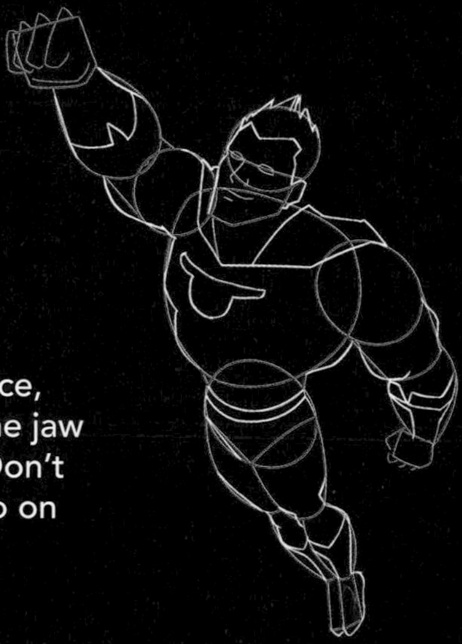

3. Add detail to the face, hair, and clothes. The jaw should be square. Don't forget to add a logo on the costume.

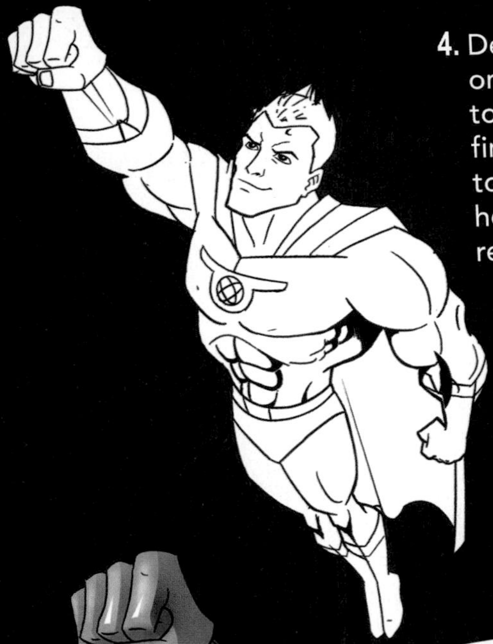

4. Define the muscles on the stomach, torso, and arms. Add finishing touches to the clothes and head. Erase any remaining guidelines.

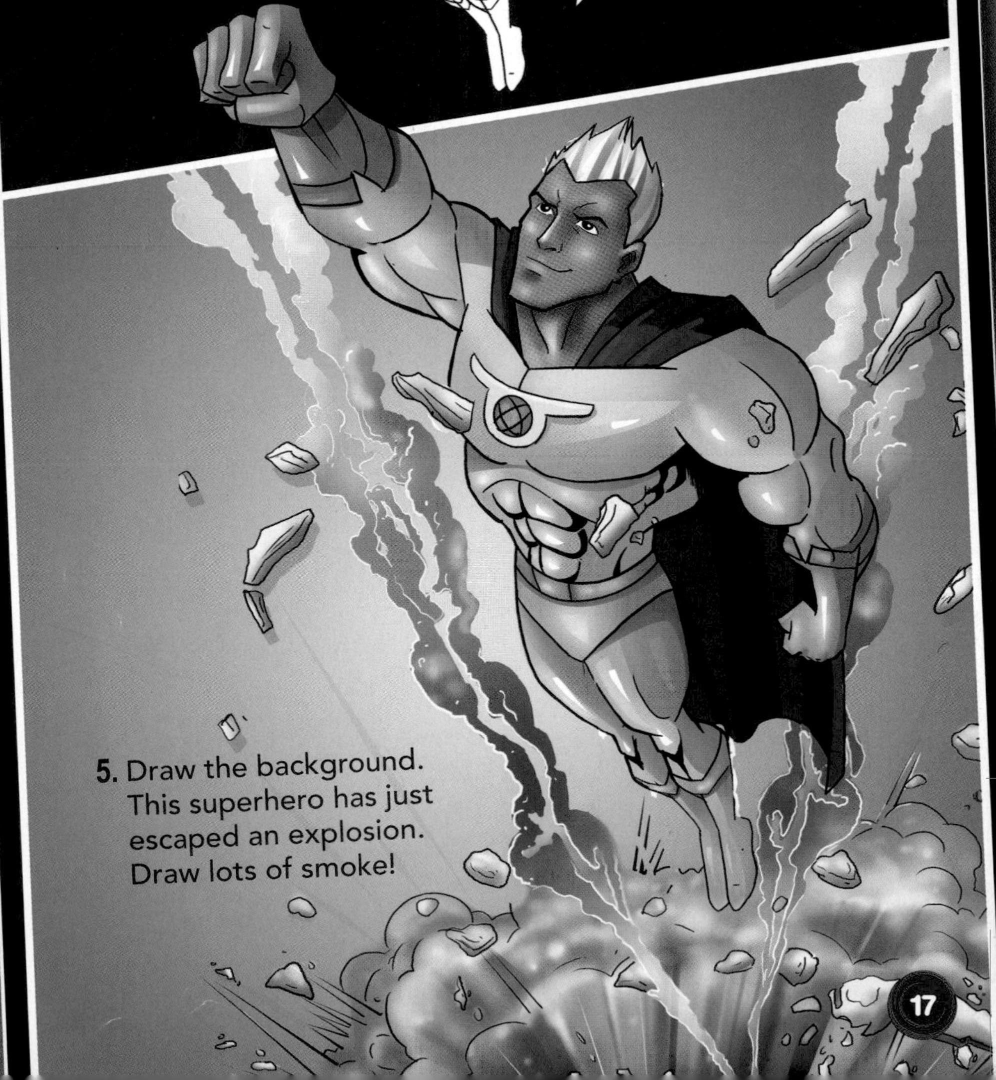

5. Draw the background. This superhero has just escaped an explosion. Draw lots of smoke!

Color Codes

You can transform a character simply by changing the colors you use. Graphic novelists often use different color schemes to bring out aspects of a character's personality or even a situation.

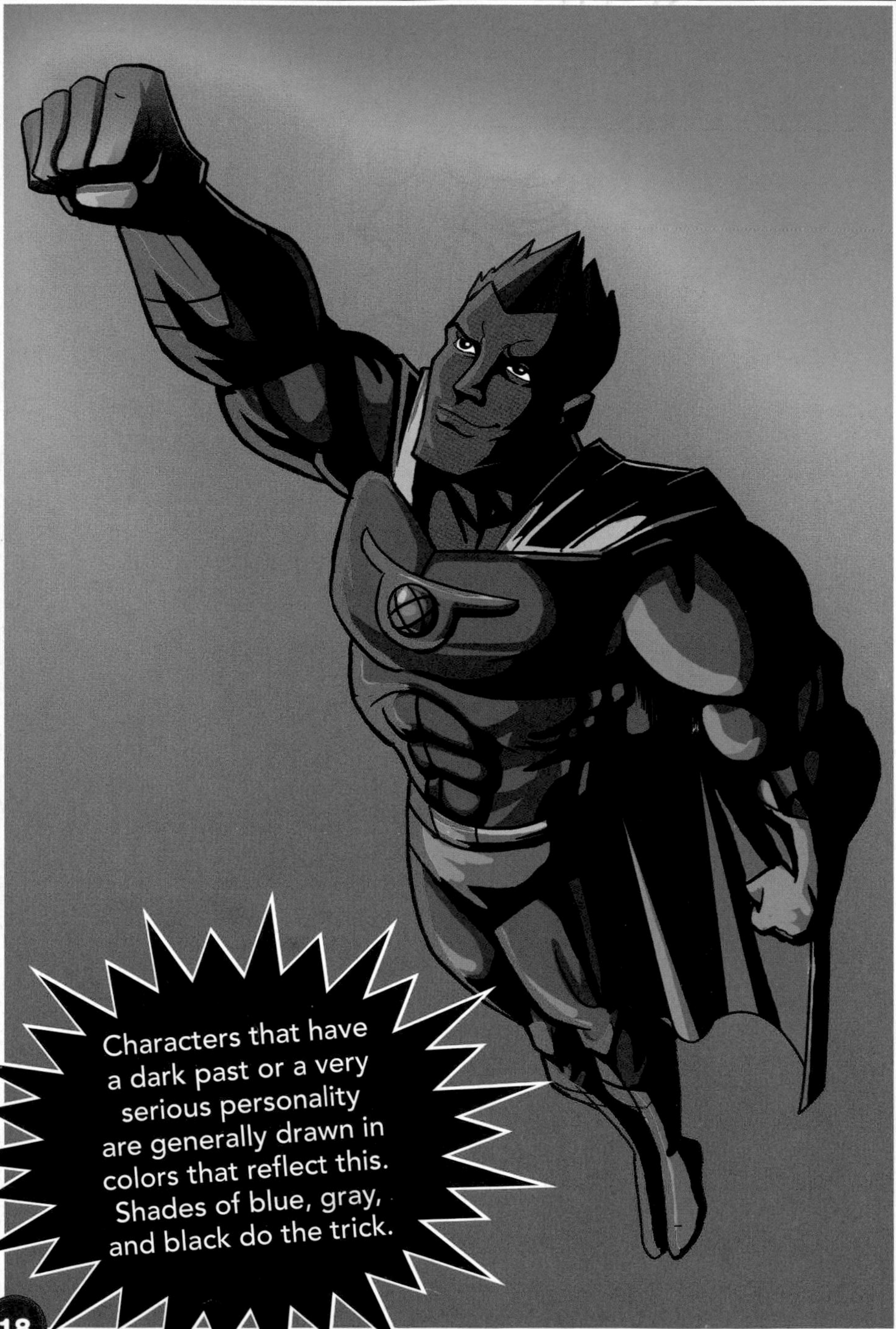

Characters that have a dark past or a very serious personality are generally drawn in colors that reflect this. Shades of blue, gray, and black do the trick.

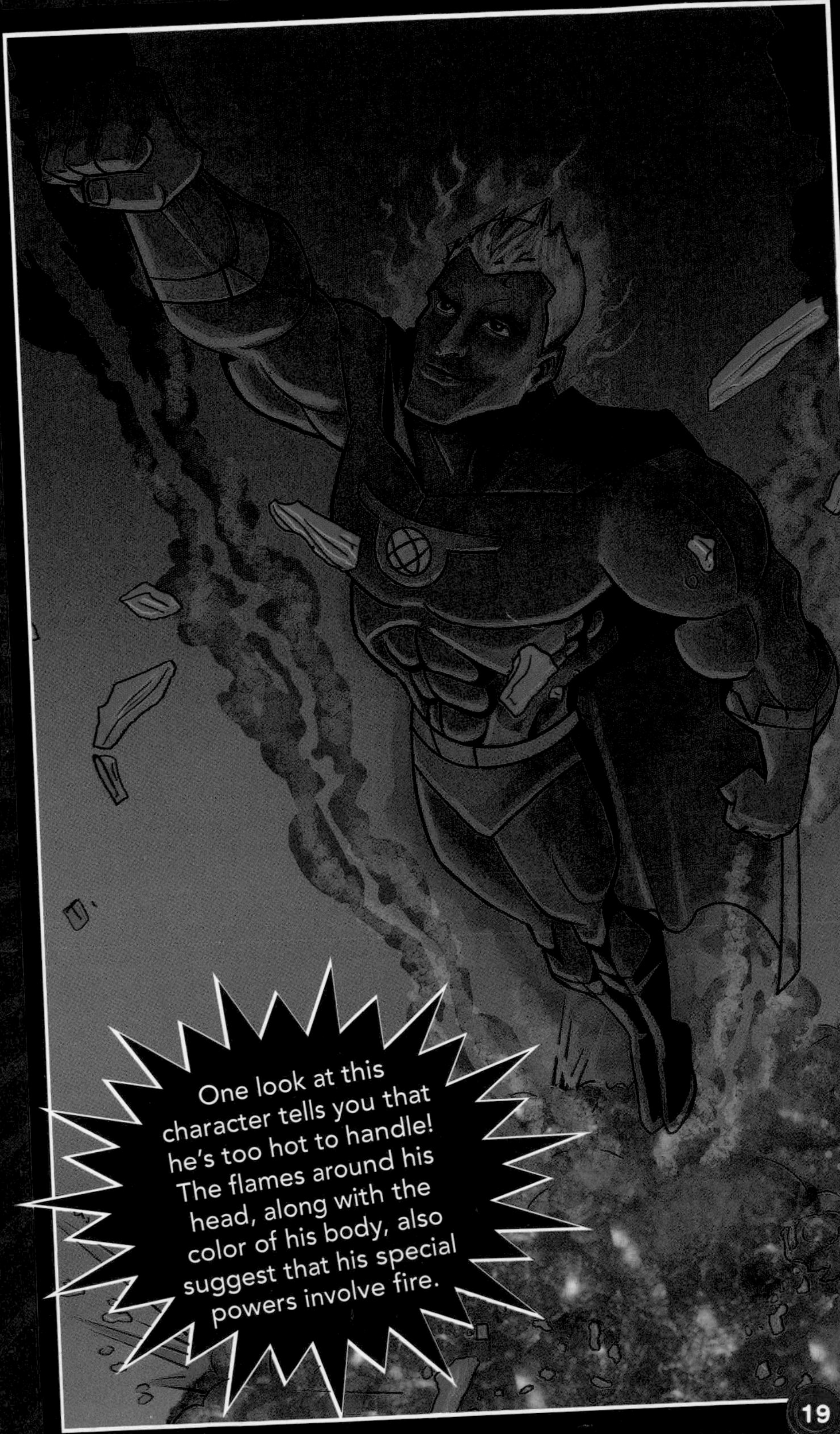
One look at this character tells you that he's too hot to handle! The flames around his head, along with the color of his body, also suggest that his special powers involve fire.

Muscle Man

He's built like a battleship, and his hands can destroy anything he touches with bolts of high-voltage energy. This superhero has no need for weapons. Bullets crumble when they hit him!

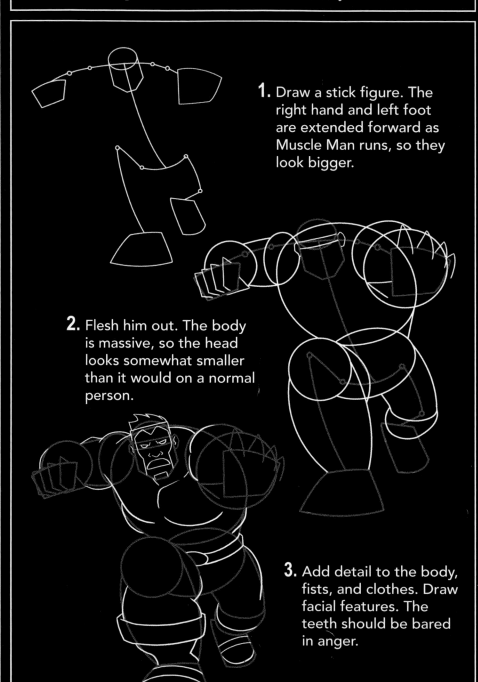

1. Draw a stick figure. The right hand and left foot are extended forward as Muscle Man runs, so they look bigger.

2. Flesh him out. The body is massive, so the head looks somewhat smaller than it would on a normal person.

3. Add detail to the body, fists, and clothes. Draw facial features. The teeth should be bared in anger.

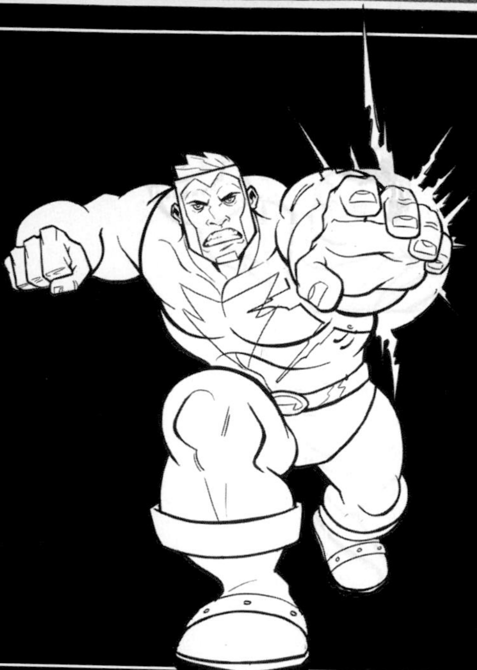

4. Draw the muscles and finish the hands and feet. The extended arm and leg should be massive. They're a preview of how scary he is up close! Draw a zig-zag shape around the hand to show bolts of energy.

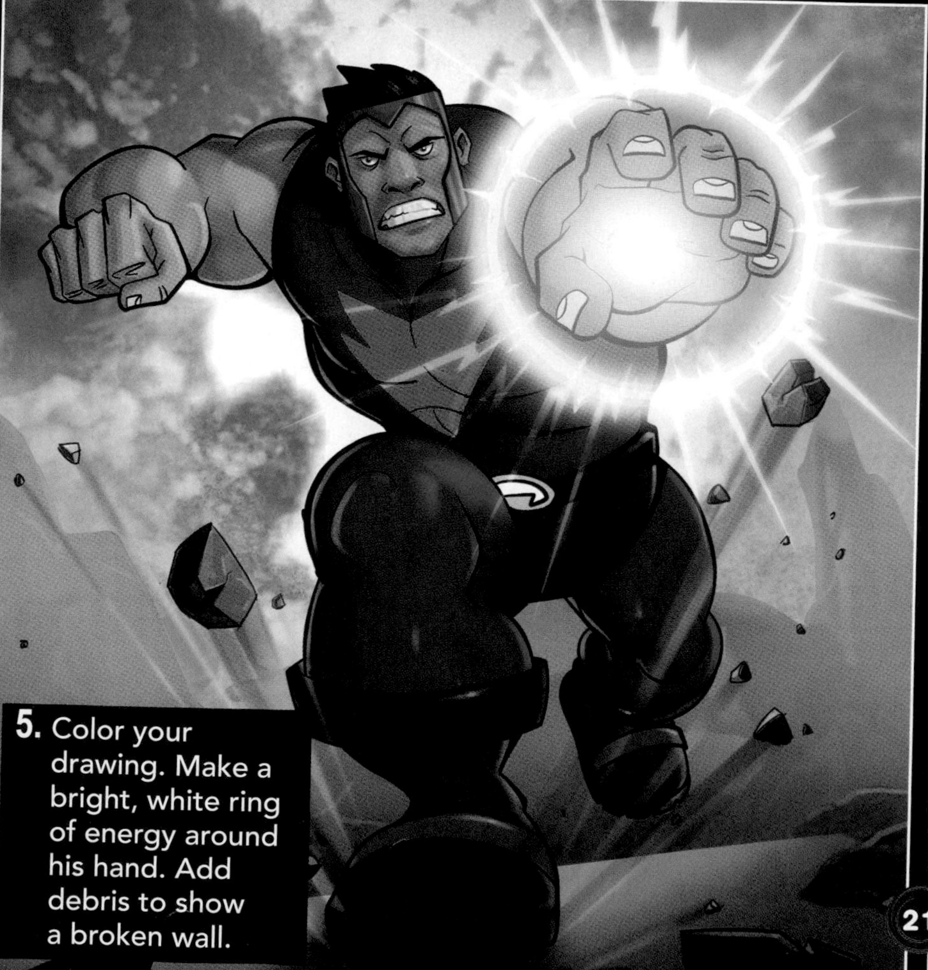

5. Color your drawing. Make a bright, white ring of energy around his hand. Add debris to show a broken wall.

Part man, part animal, part stone, and all mutant superhero. A military experiment in a secret jungle turned one arm to super-strong stone and one hand into a massive claw. His job is to hunt for terrorists hiding in dangerous forests. He crashes through giant boulders and scares off wild animals.

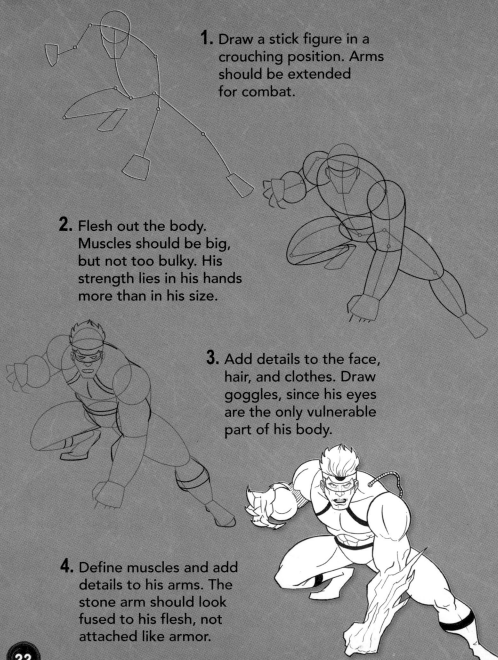

1. Draw a stick figure in a crouching position. Arms should be extended for combat.

2. Flesh out the body. Muscles should be big, but not too bulky. His strength lies in his hands more than in his size.

3. Add details to the face, hair, and clothes. Draw goggles, since his eyes are the only vulnerable part of his body.

4. Define muscles and add details to his arms. The stone arm should look fused to his flesh, not attached like armor.

5. Draw a setting. The Jungle Mutant has just broken into a terrorist group's mountain hideout.

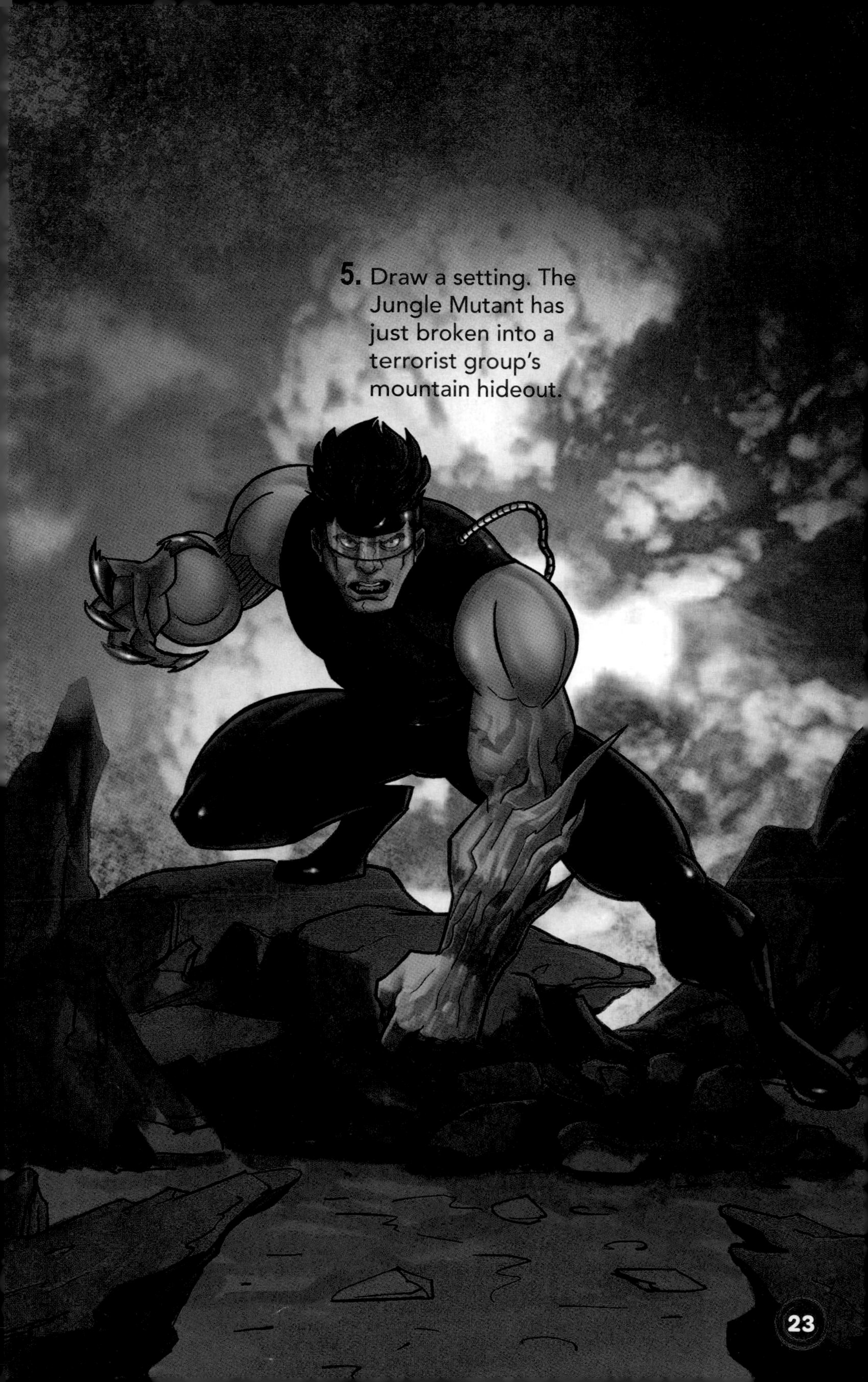

CHAPTER 6

POWER WOMEN

Superheroines don't need big muscles to squash their enemies. Their brains, toughness, agility, and special abilities help them beat most odds.

Sonic Bloom

A special power makes fighting villains easier. Give your superheroine something unique, like the ability to shoot sonic waves from her hands! A tight latex costume makes it easy to run and jump. And bright colors add a feminine touch.

1. Start with a stick figure. Give her a dynamic pose and don't forget to make her "attacking" hand larger than the other.

2. Flesh out the body. Remember to make her waist smaller than her shoulders and hips.

3. Let her hair flow behind her. Draw in an outline of clothes and a face.

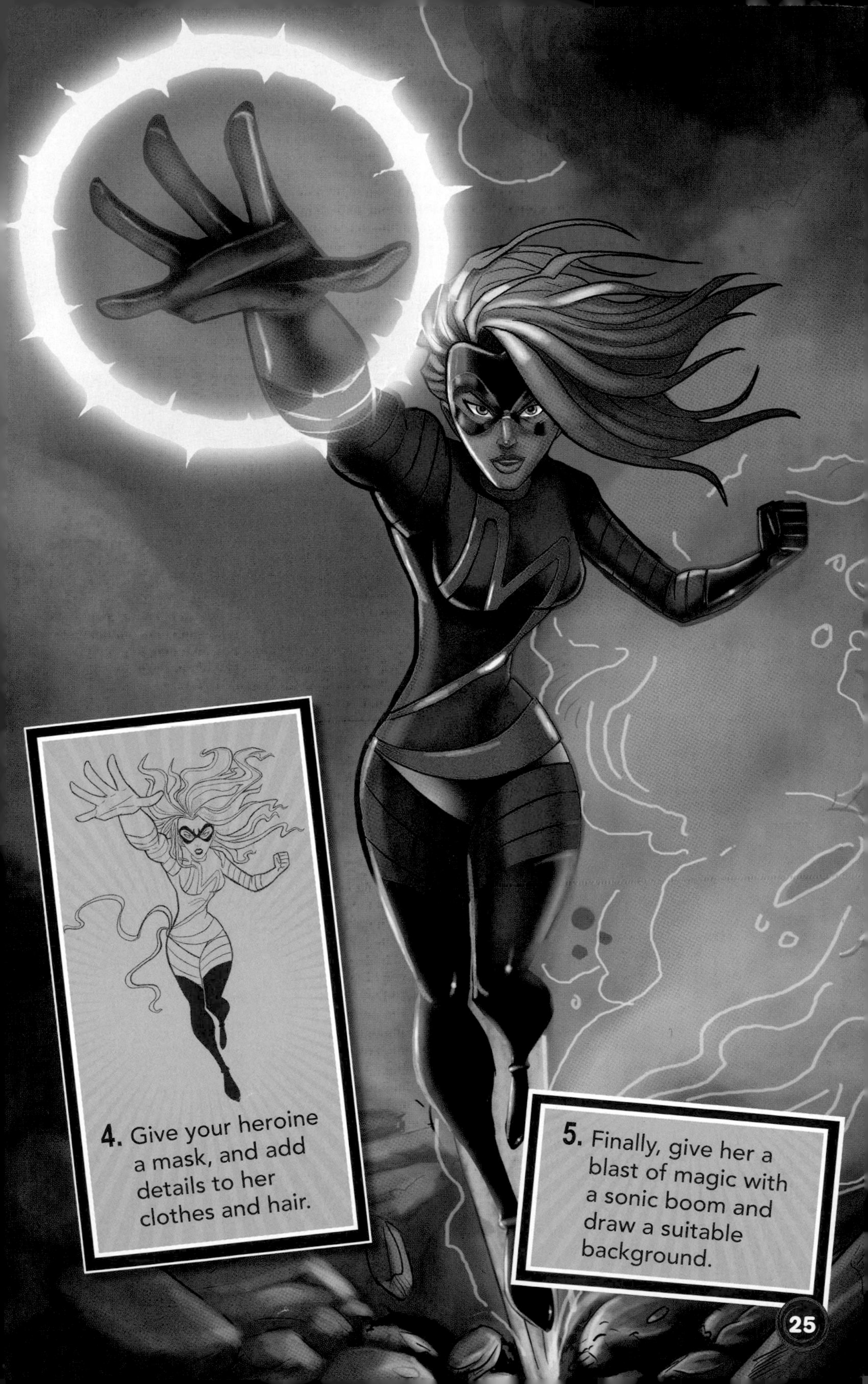

4. Give your heroine a mask, and add details to her clothes and hair.

5. Finally, give her a blast of magic with a sonic boom and draw a suitable background.

Not all superheroines have superpowers. Sometimes, all it takes is the will, the right attitude, and a whole lot of martial arts training.

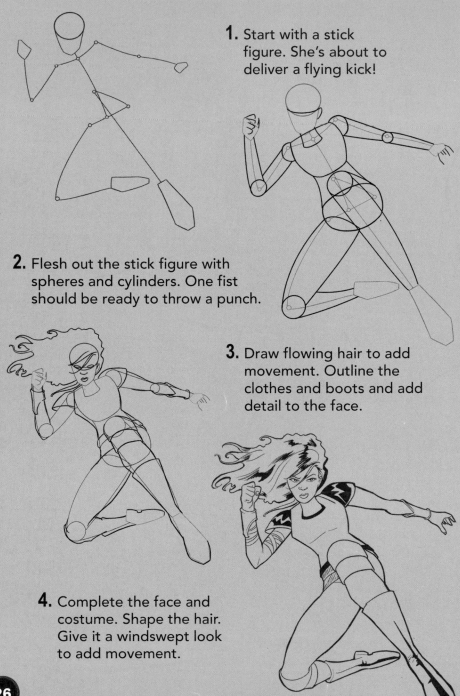

1. Start with a stick figure. She's about to deliver a flying kick!

2. Flesh out the stick figure with spheres and cylinders. One fist should be ready to throw a punch.

3. Draw flowing hair to add movement. Outline the clothes and boots and add detail to the face.

4. Complete the face and costume. Shape the hair. Give it a windswept look to add movement.

5. Add a background so she looks like she's in the middle of knocking out the bad guys in a deserted alley.

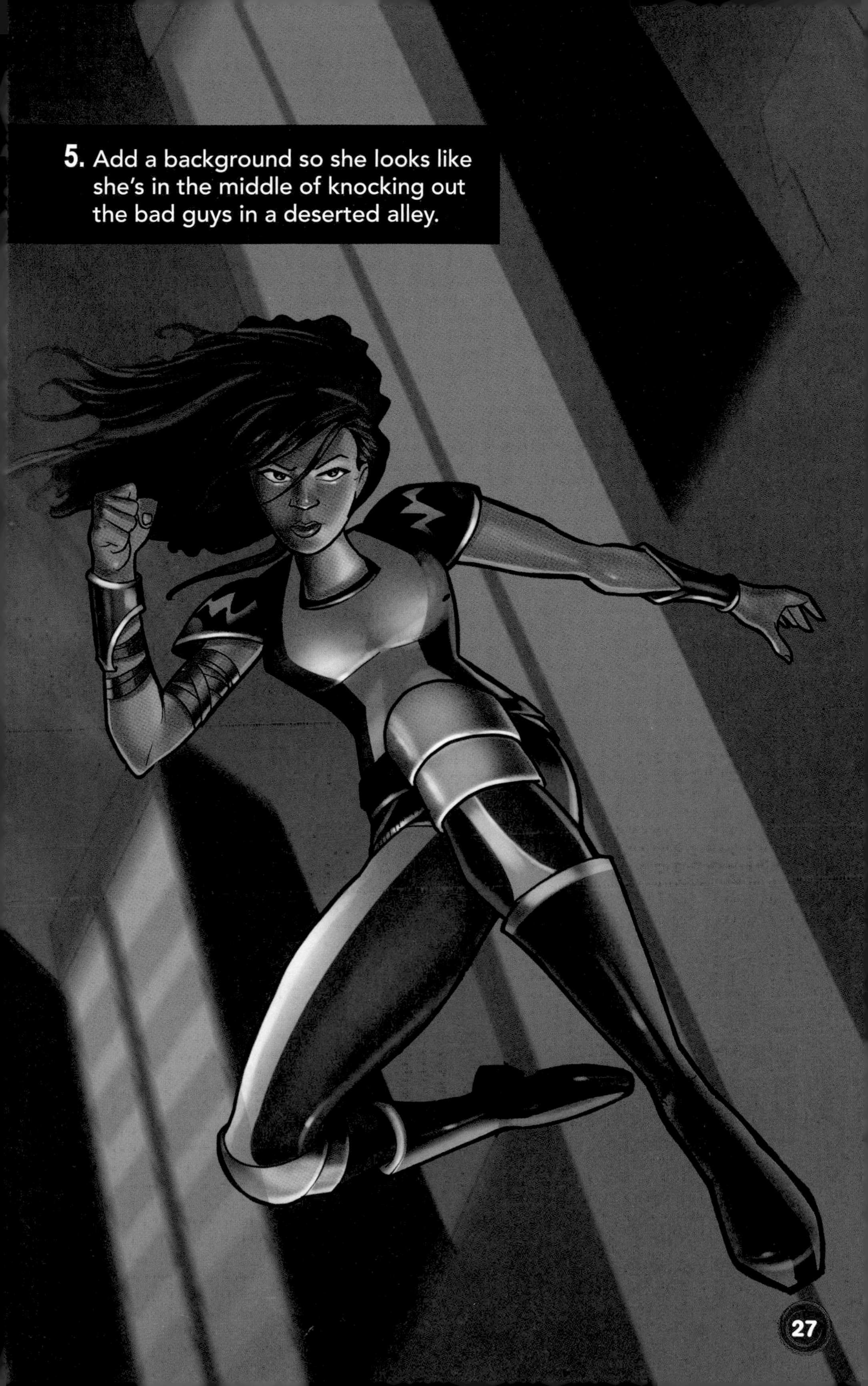

CHAPTER 7

SUPERVILLAINS

They're evil, they're repulsive, and they wouldn't have it any other way. Villains are what make superheroes' lives interesting.

Dr V: Vision Vandal

Many villains start off as good guys, who then go bad. Dr. V was a hypnotherapist before he became a hypnothera-pest. He uses mind control and special powers in his hands to steal people's vision.

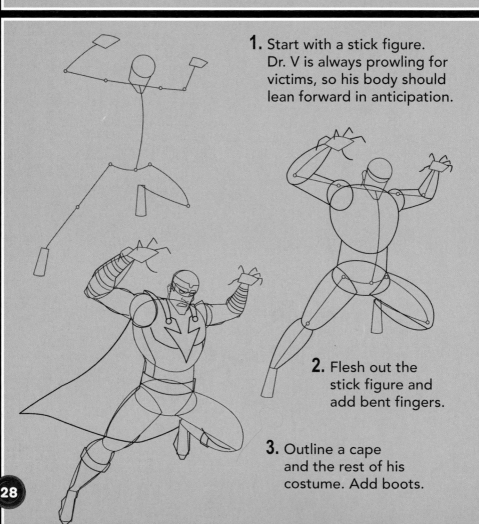

1. Start with a stick figure. Dr. V is always prowling for victims, so his body should lean forward in anticipation.

2. Flesh out the stick figure and add bent fingers.

3. Outline a cape and the rest of his costume. Add boots.

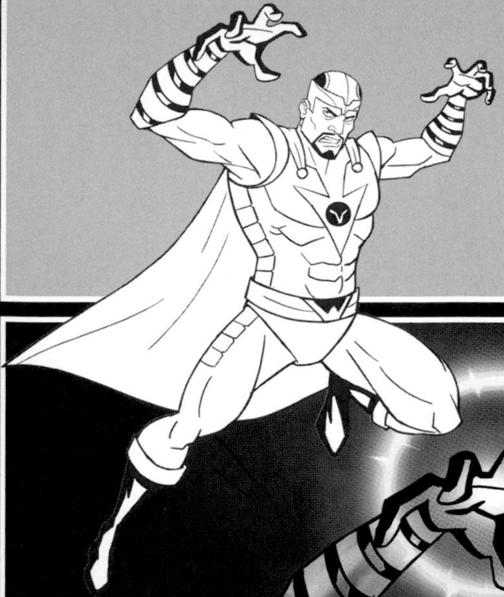

4. Complete the face, muscles, and costume. Don't forget to give him an evil snarl.

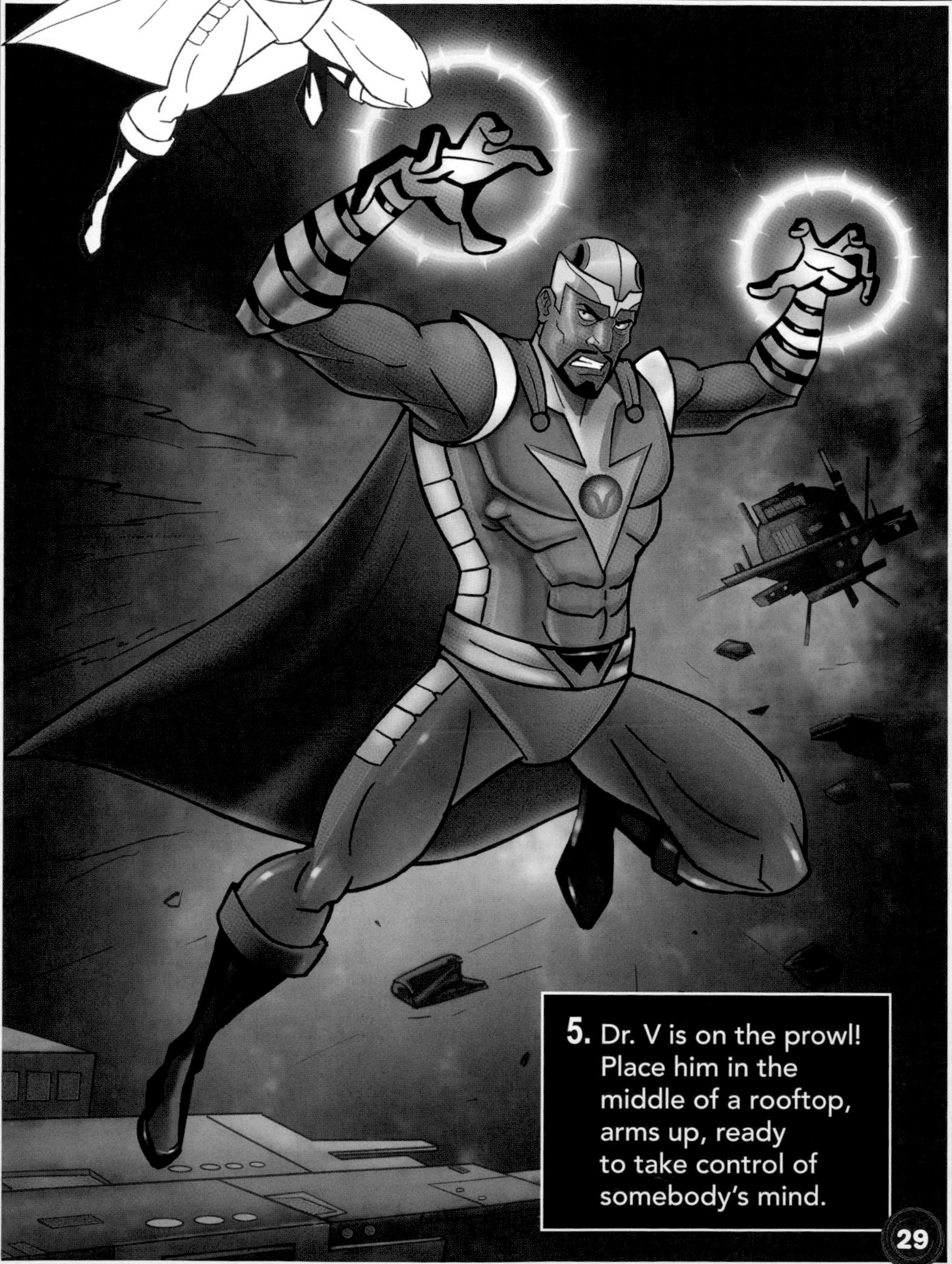

5. Dr. V is on the prowl! Place him in the middle of a rooftop, arms up, ready to take control of somebody's mind.

Bionic Beast

Bionic Beast lost an arm and half his face in a biochemical accident. Since then he's been in a bad mood and is taking it out on the world.

1. Start with a stick figure. Villains are always heading toward trouble in new ways, so he should look like he's flying forward.

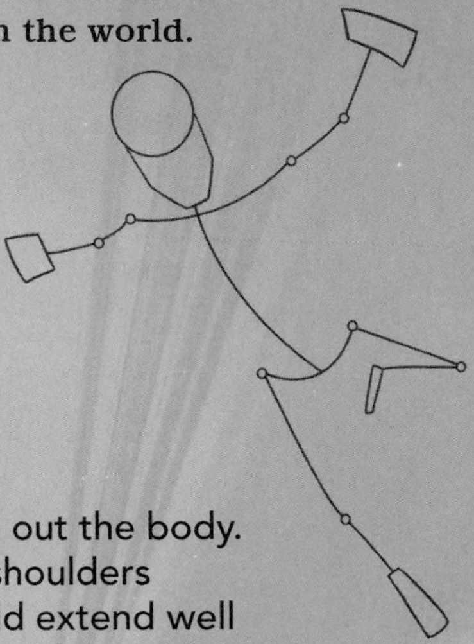

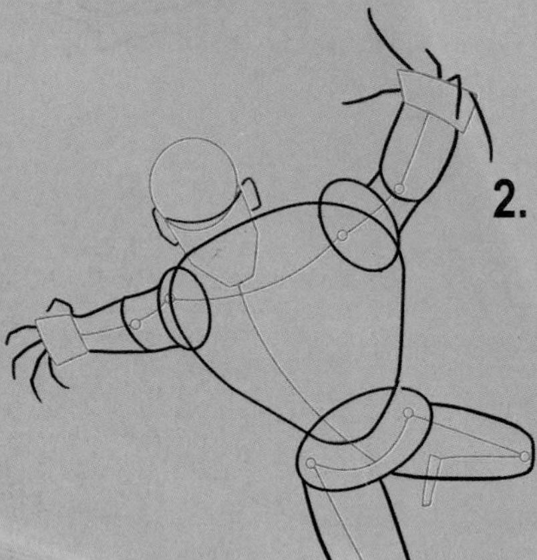

2. Flesh out the body. The shoulders should extend well behind the head.

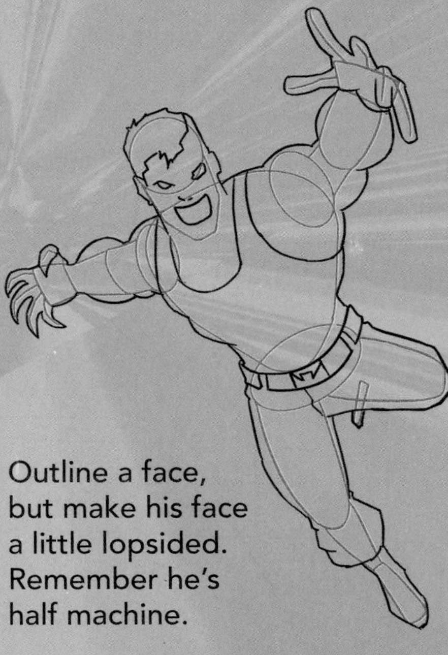

3. Outline a face, but make his face a little lopsided. Remember he's half machine.

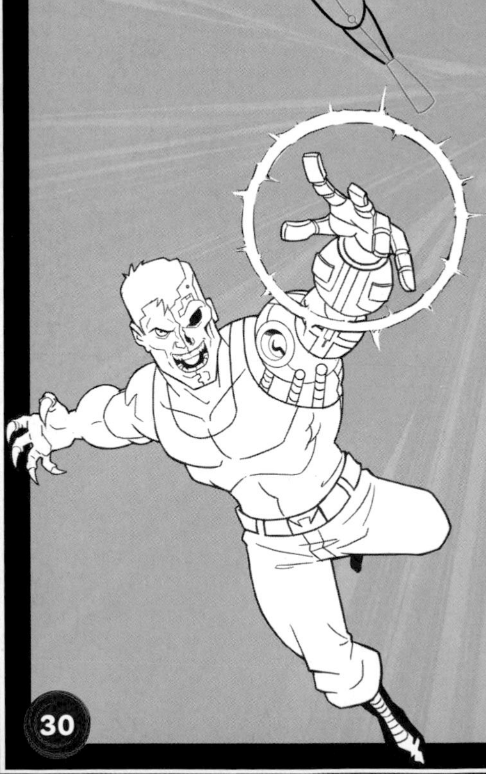

4. Draw his clothes and give him an angry expression. Add details to his bionic arm.

5. Color the Bionic Beast. One side of his face and one arm should look metallic.

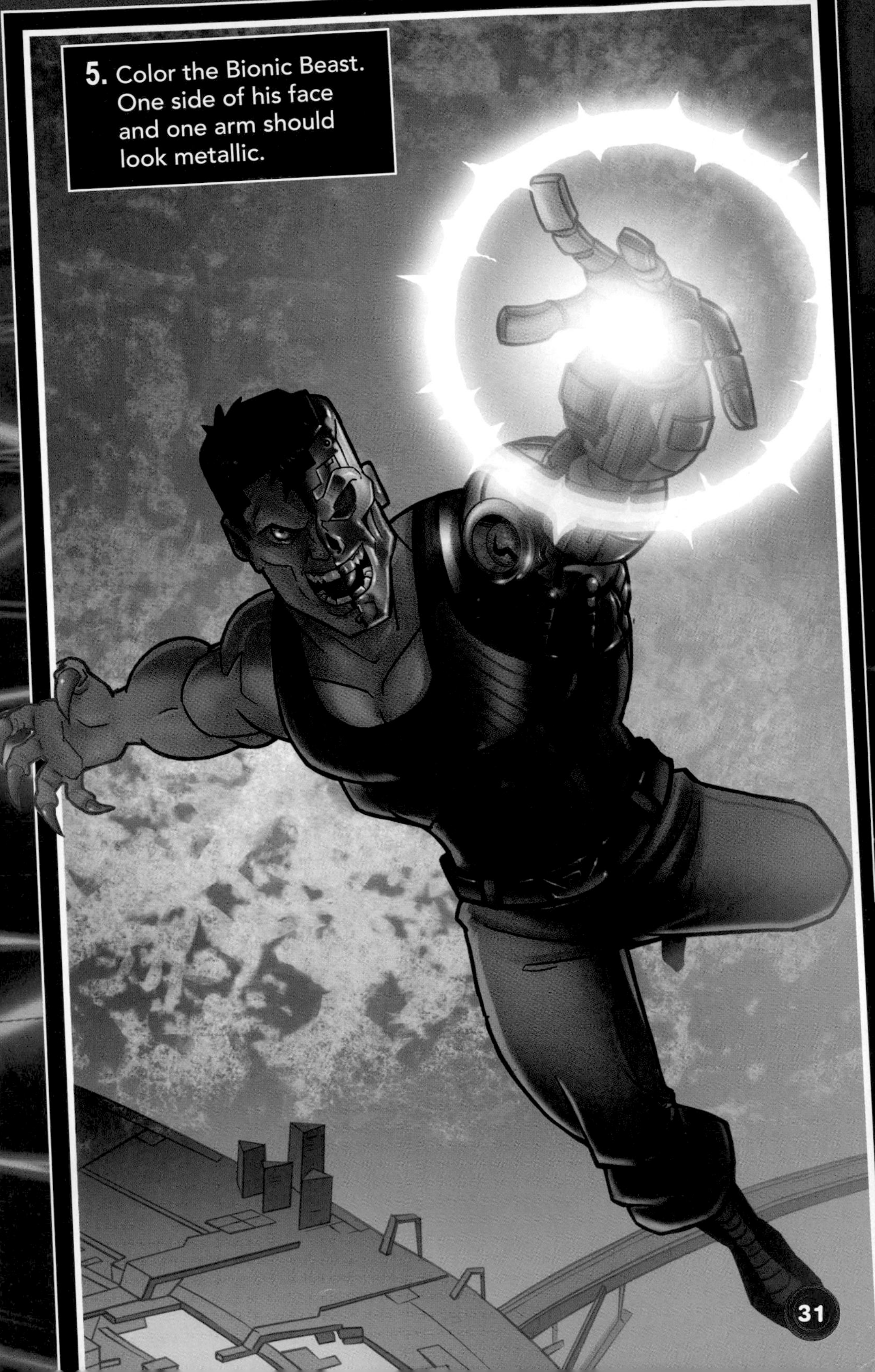

Lizardo

Sometimes in the world of comics, people turn into creatures. Lizardo worked in a junkyard until radioactive waste made him toxic.

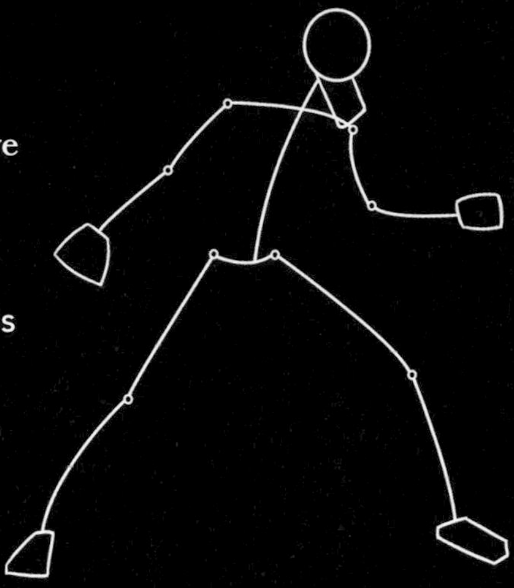

1. Start with a stick figure. Lizards are long and skinny, so make Lizardo thin and lanky.

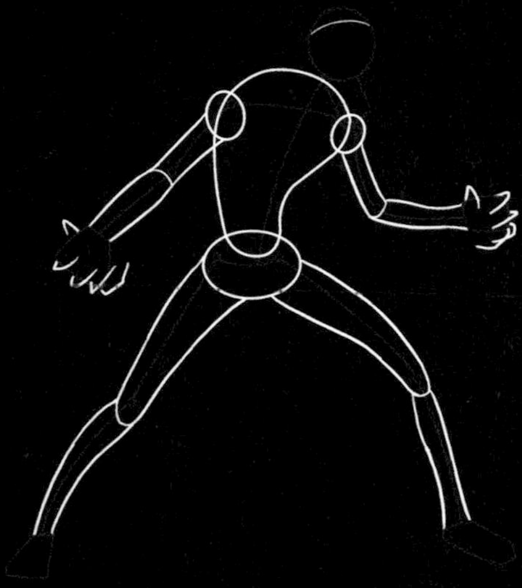

2. Flesh out the body. Lizardo is tall, thin, and slithery.

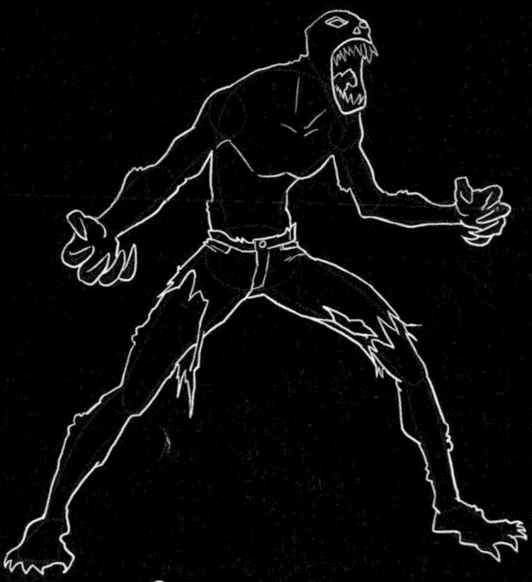

3. Draw details of leftover rags, scary teeth, and claws.

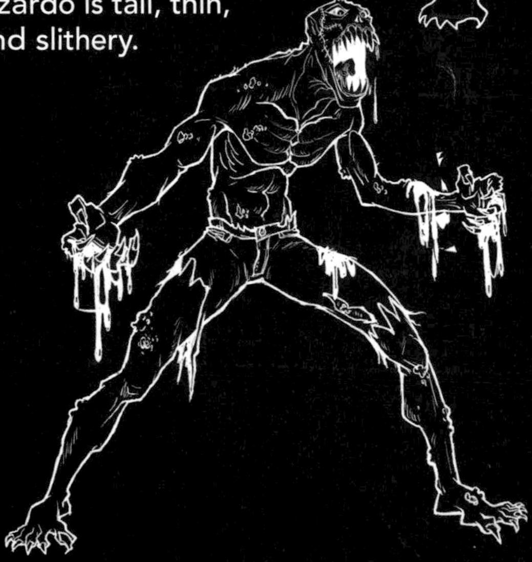

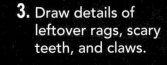

4. Add details to his body and rags. Make him drool, and add some gross slime sticking to him.

5. Lizardo is soaking up energy from the toxic green waste in a lab's dumping ground. Draw a ruined barbed wire fence in the background.

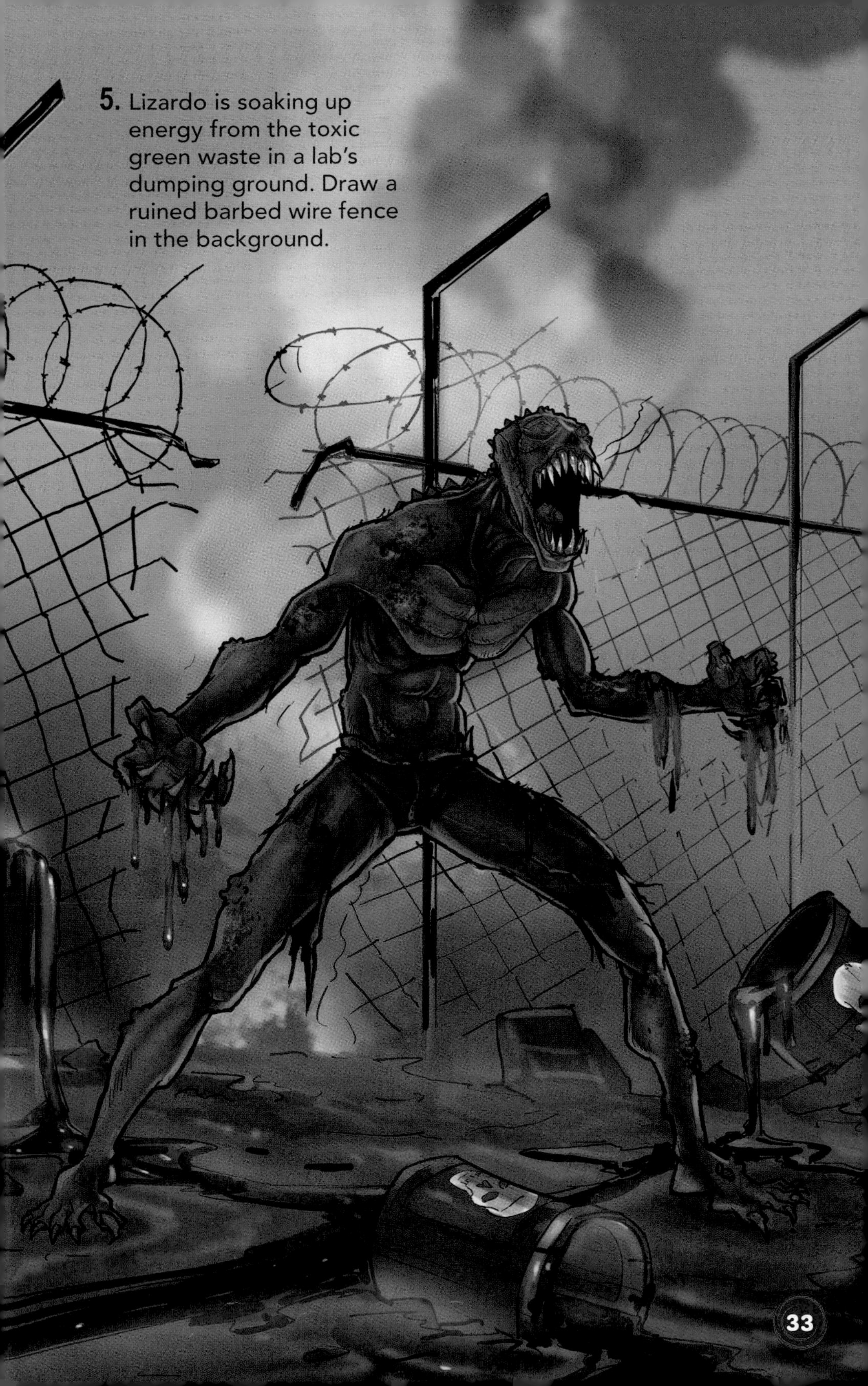

Lady Nightshade

Watch out for this woman. She's pure poison, like the plant she's named after.

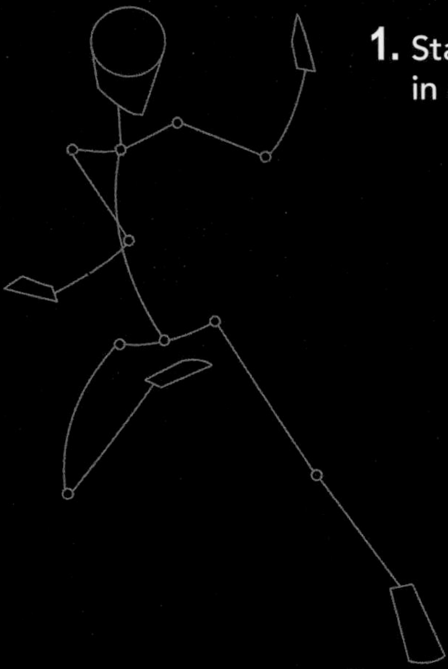

1. Start with a stick figure in an action pose.

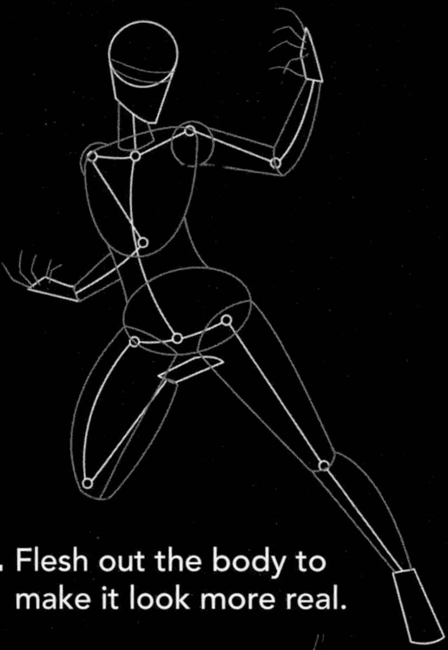

2. Flesh out the body to make it look more real.

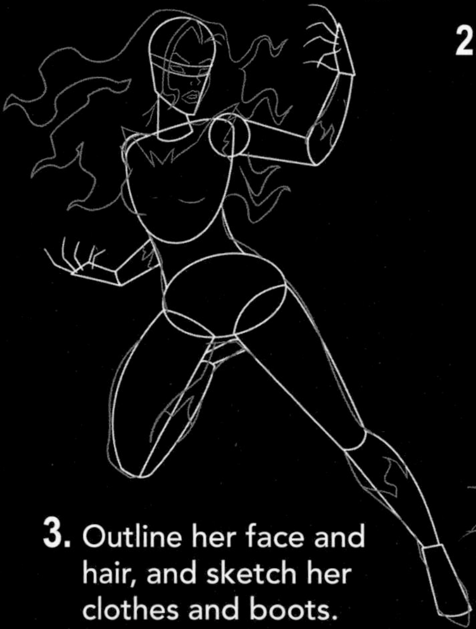

3. Outline her face and hair, and sketch her clothes and boots.

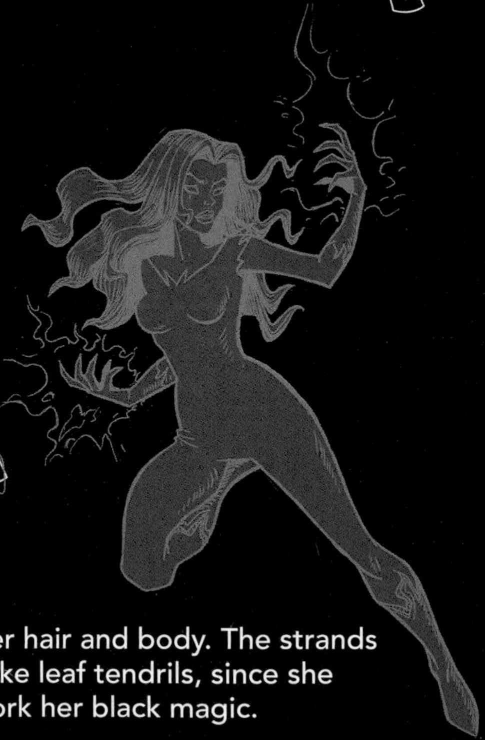

4. Add details to her hair and body. The strands of her hair look like leaf tendrils, since she uses plants to work her black magic.

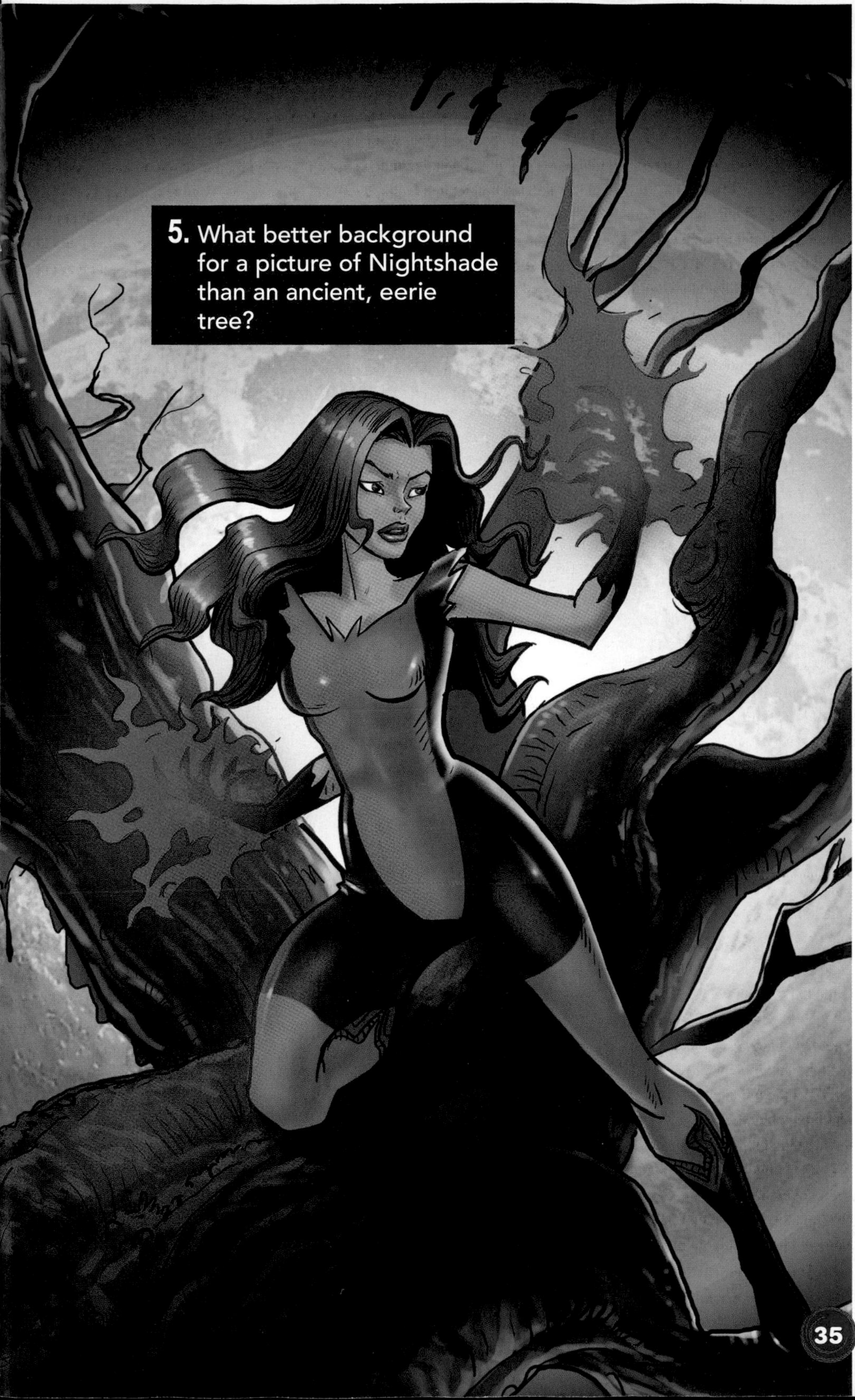

5. What better background for a picture of Nightshade than an ancient, eerie tree?

CHAPTER 8

SETTING THE SCENE

Since graphic novels are meant to be read, and yet have limited space for words, settings can tell you a lot about the character and the story.

Points of View

Comic panels work a lot like camera shots. They show scenes and people from different angles. Each shot highlights different aspects of the story.

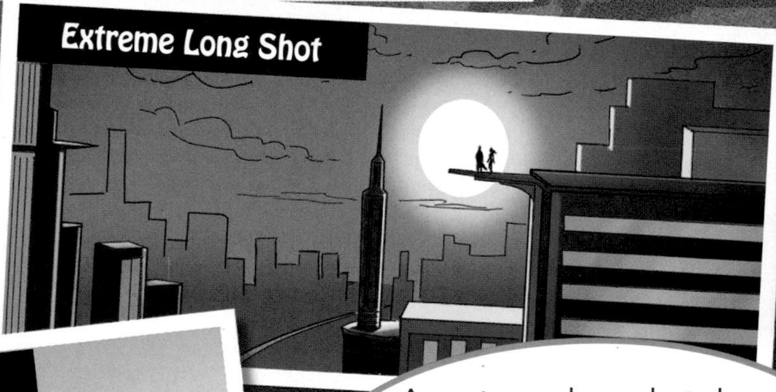

Extreme Long Shot

An extreme long shot shows scenes from a distance. It presents a broad view of a large setting, like a city or countryside.

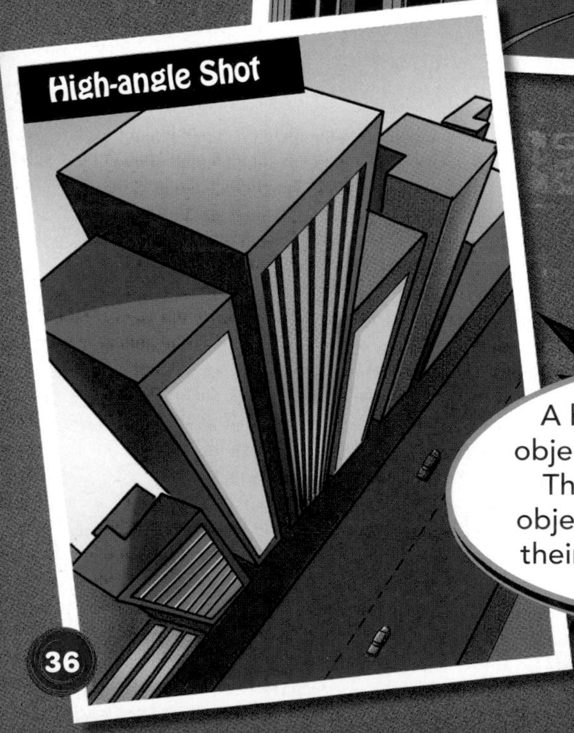

High-angle Shot

A high-angle shot captures objects or a scene from above. They help show the size of objects (like cars) in relation to their surroundings (buildings).

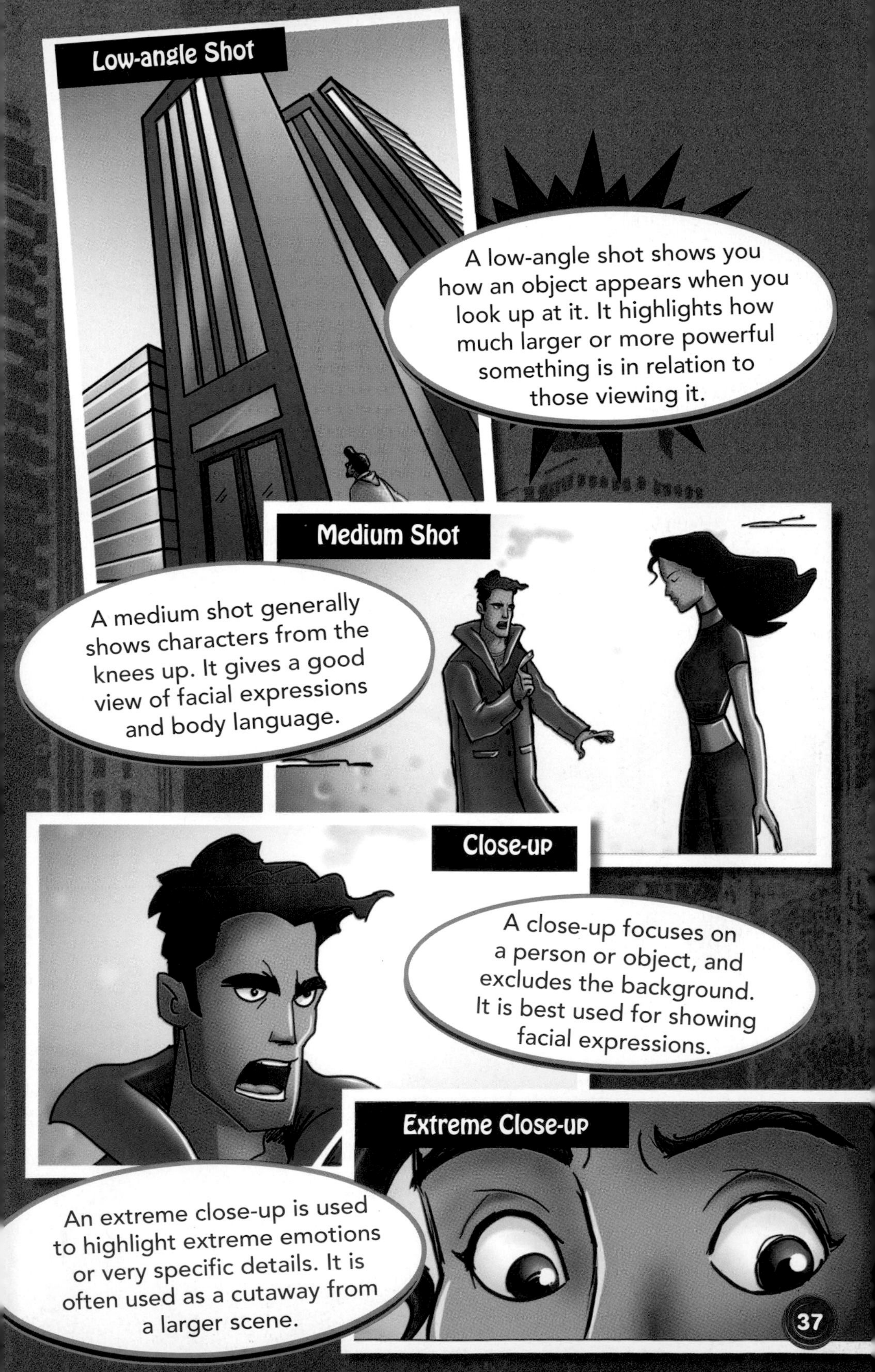
Low-angle Shot
A low-angle shot shows you how an object appears when you look up at it. It highlights how much larger or more powerful something is in relation to those viewing it.
Medium Shot
A medium shot generally shows characters from the knees up. It gives a good view of facial expressions and body language.
Close-up
A close-up focuses on a person or object, and excludes the background. It is best used for showing facial expressions.
Extreme Close-up
An extreme close-up is used to highlight extreme emotions or very specific details. It is often used as a cutaway from a larger scene.

Where and When

The background of a panel tells a story too. Every scene unfolds in a particular setting, such as a dark alley, cafeteria, basement, or spaceship. You can also create a mood or atmosphere by setting your scene at a particular time of day or season.

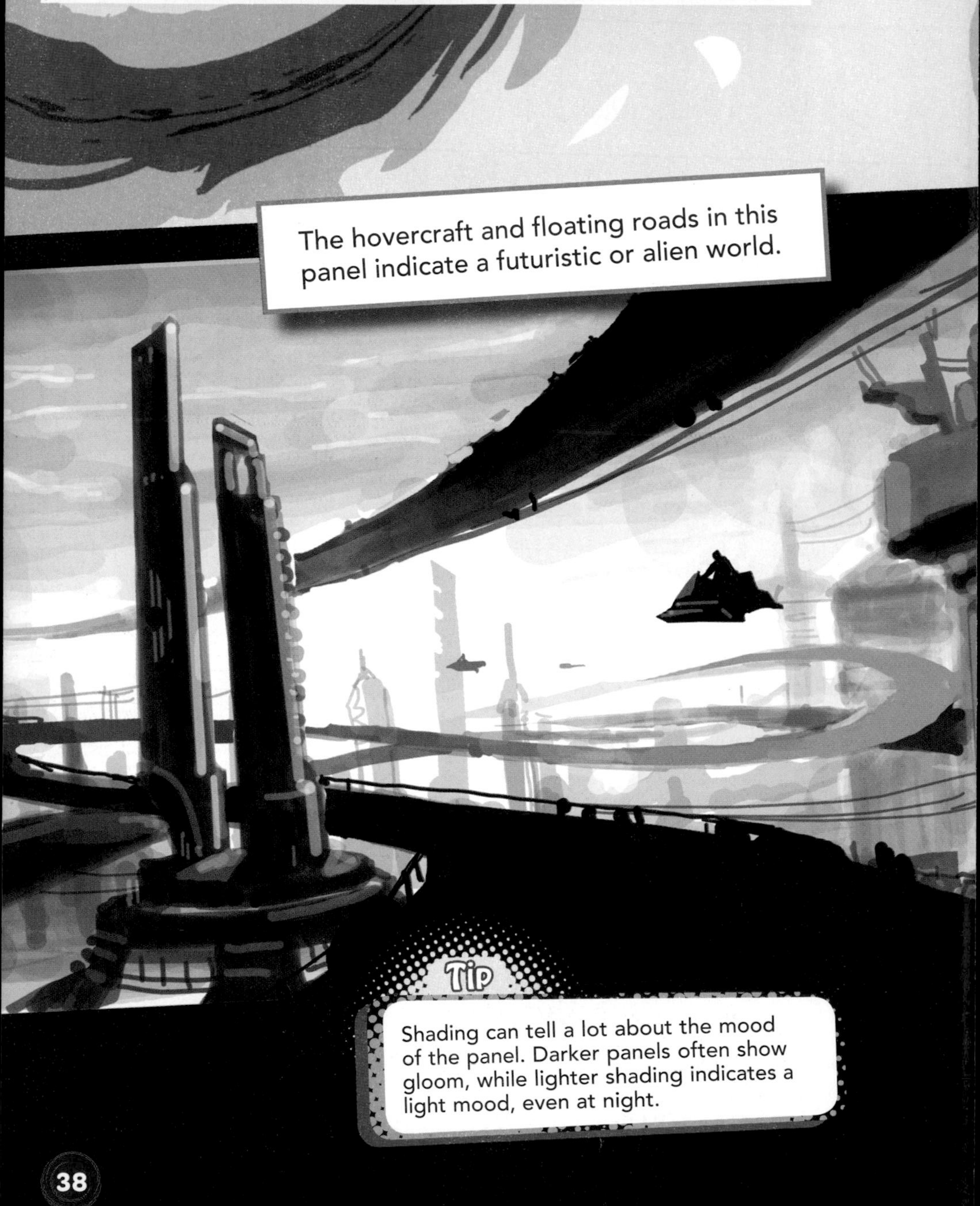

The hovercraft and floating roads in this panel indicate a futuristic or alien world.

Tip

Shading can tell a lot about the mood of the panel. Darker panels often show gloom, while lighter shading indicates a light mood, even at night.

Note how the single shaft of light brings the lone man into focus. This dark, brooding panel of an alley at night would fit in with a horror story, a mystery, or even a spy thriller.

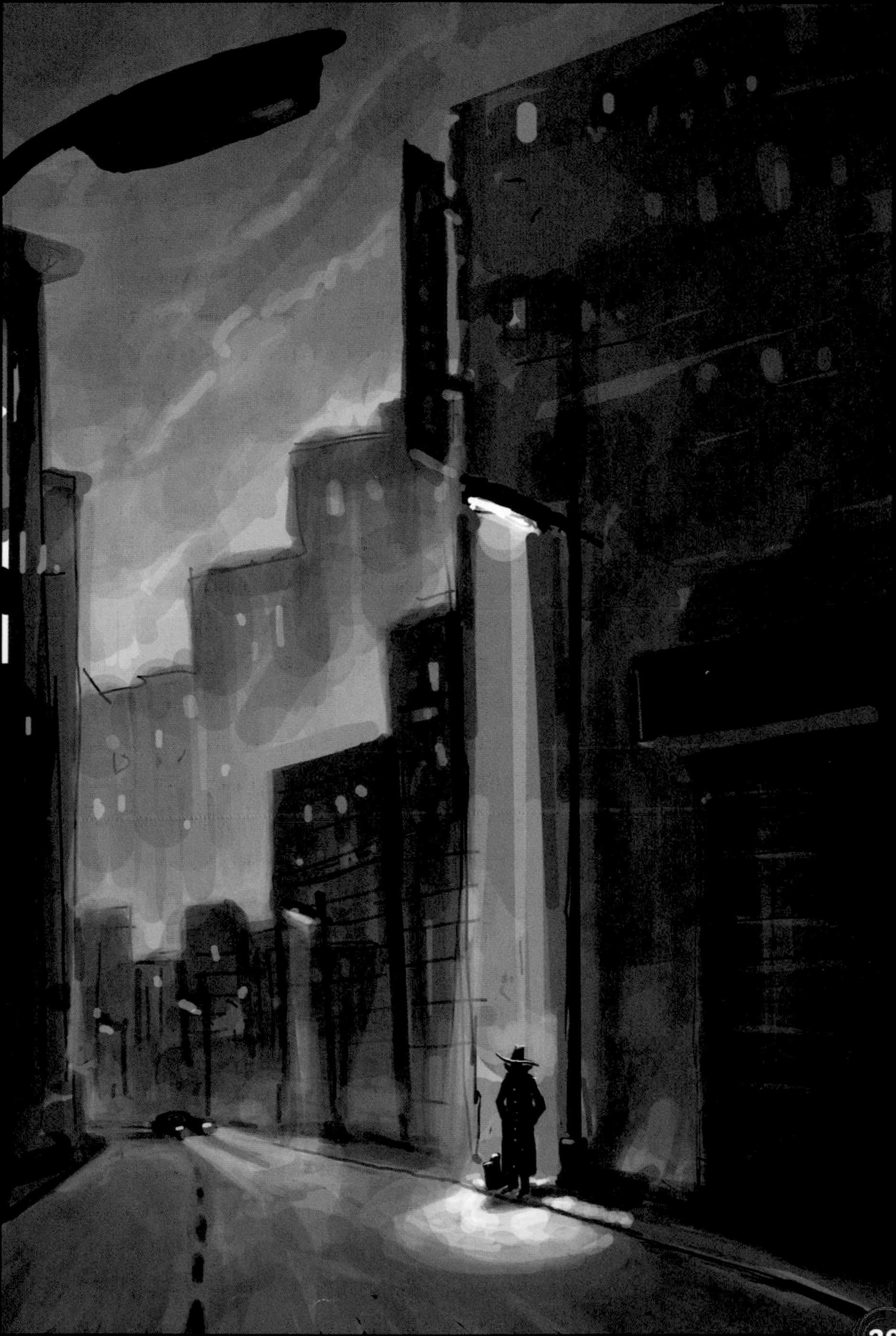

Pull-Out Punch

If your art looks good on paper, chances are it would look just as great up on your wall. Colorful pull-out posters are a comic book tradition. So, make your own! Try drawing your strongest characters against a bold background. Or, make a series of panels. This poster is about Kung-fu Manda's epic fight against four very different villains.

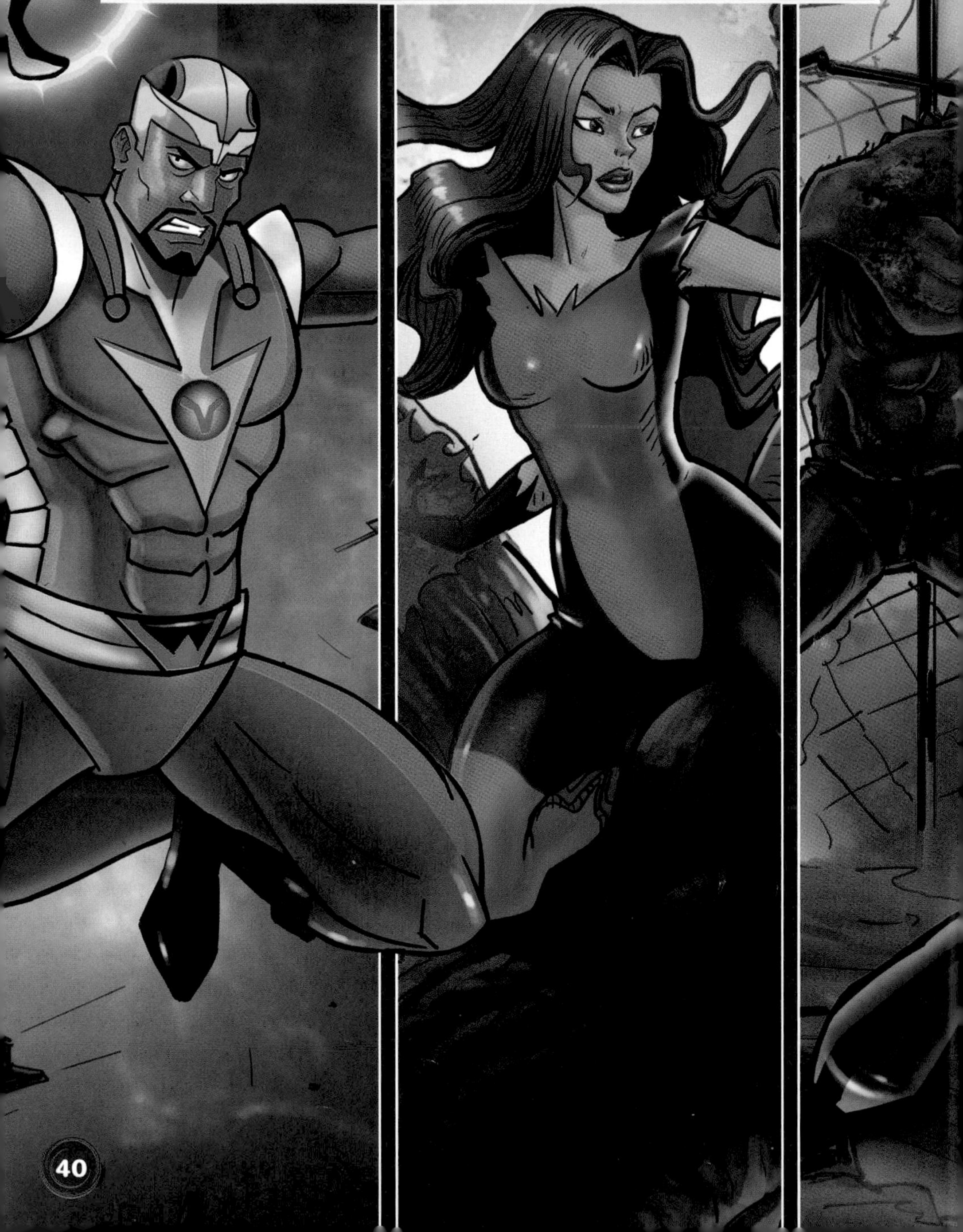

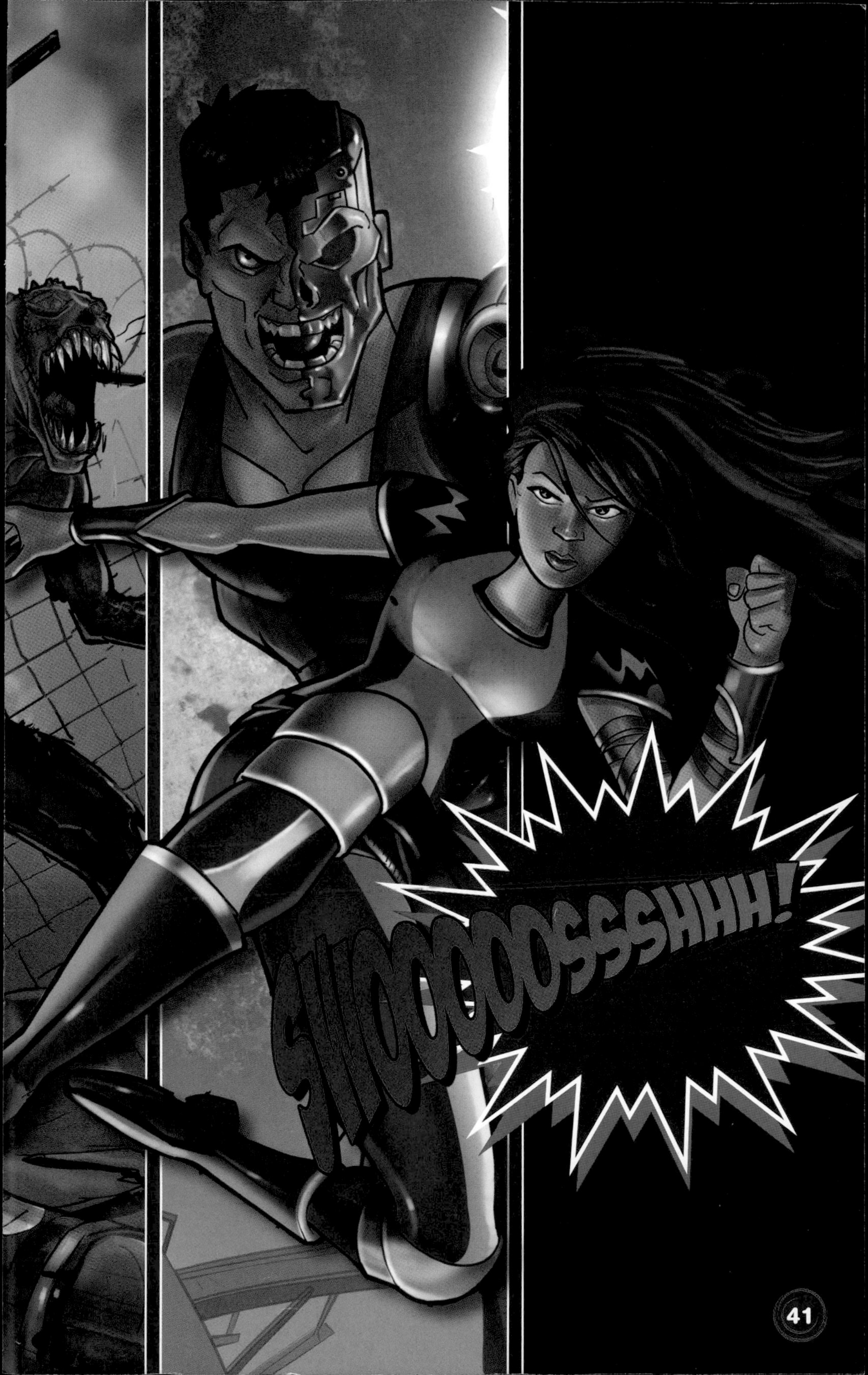
SHOOOOOOSSSSHHH!

CHAPTER 9

MAKING A STORY

Once you've thought up a plot and characters, bring them to life with your pen. Just follow these steps.

Figured out how you want your page to look? The first step is to make a storyboard, or a sequence of panels with rough sketches.

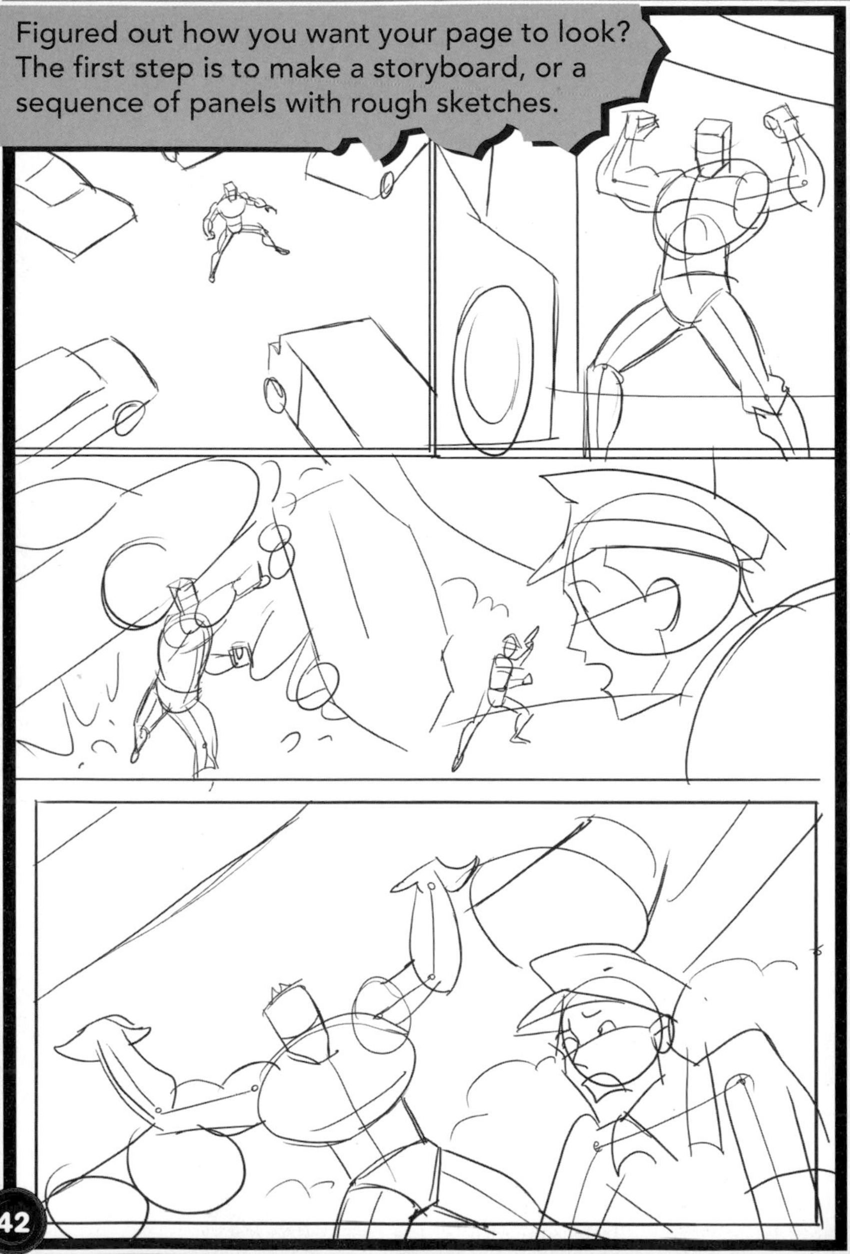

One page could have many panels. Different panels can show different points of view. They can be different shapes and sizes, depending on what you want to focus on.

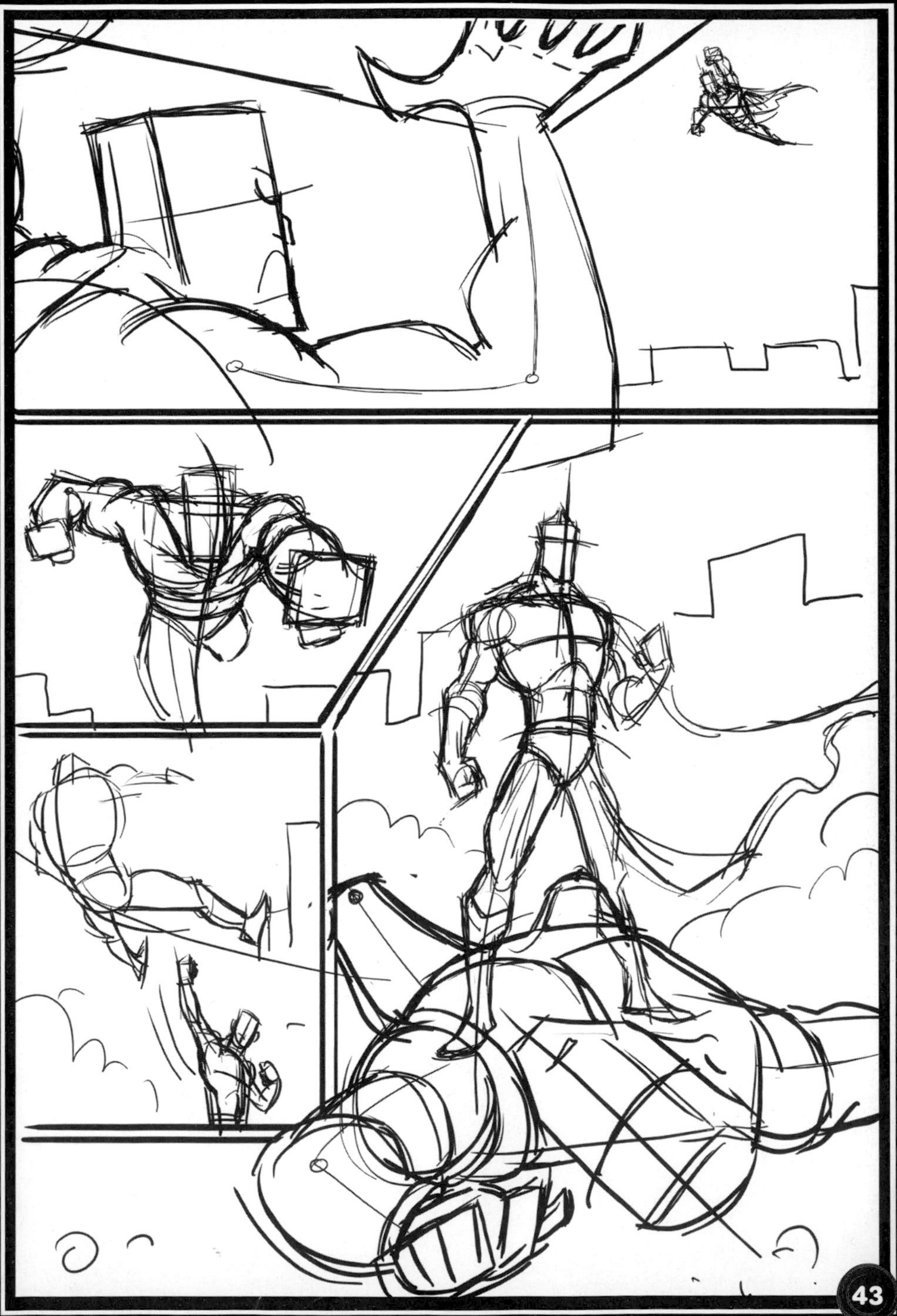

Complete your sketches and color them. This sequence shows a villain on a rampage against law enforcement. It's clear that the poor cops are no match for the bad-tempered Bionic Beast!

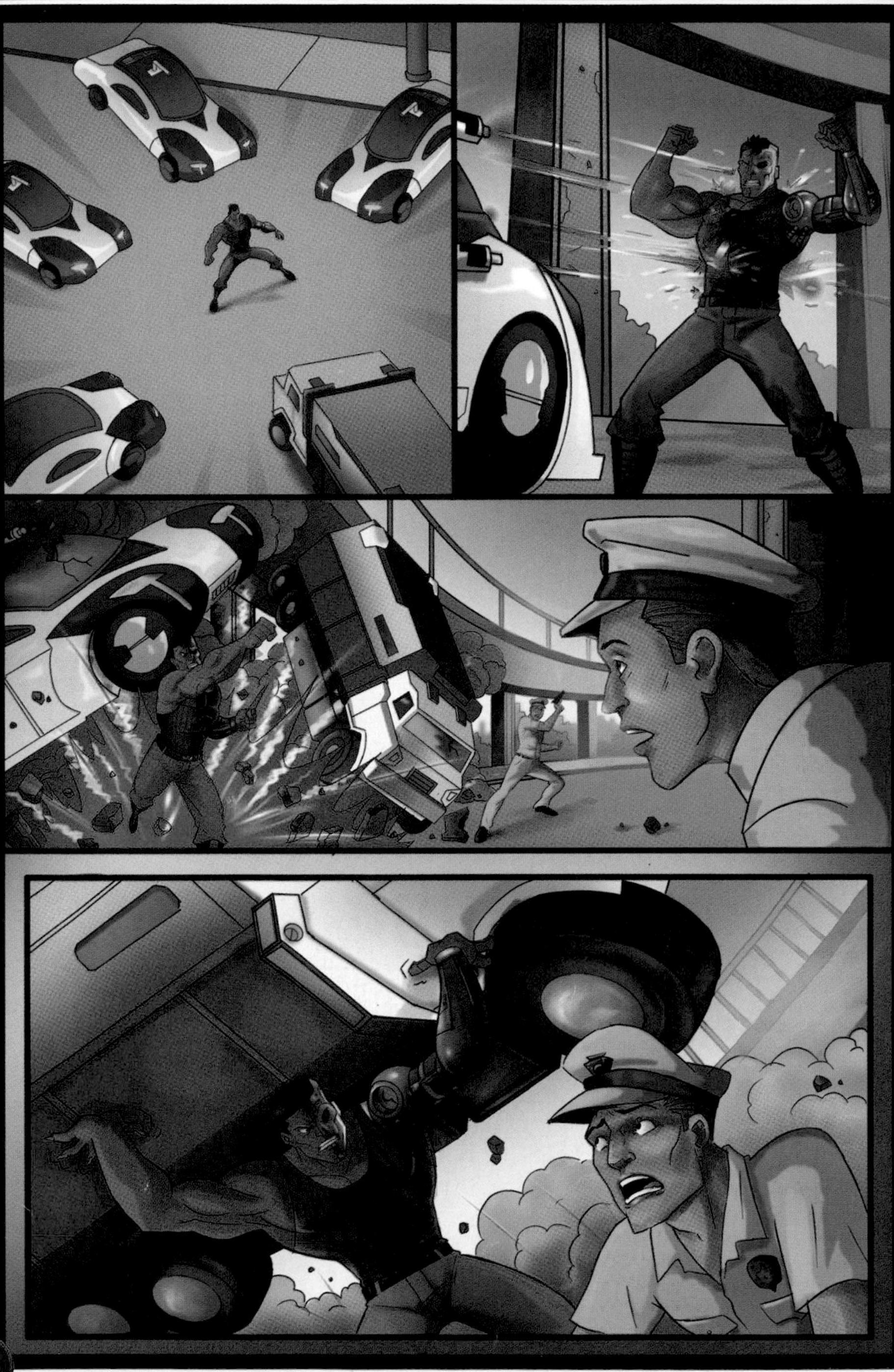

But there's a change of plans! The Caped Avenger comes to the rescue! The first two panels on this page show the superhero from the villain's point of view. The last two panels show both characters in action— or in the case of the villain, out of action.

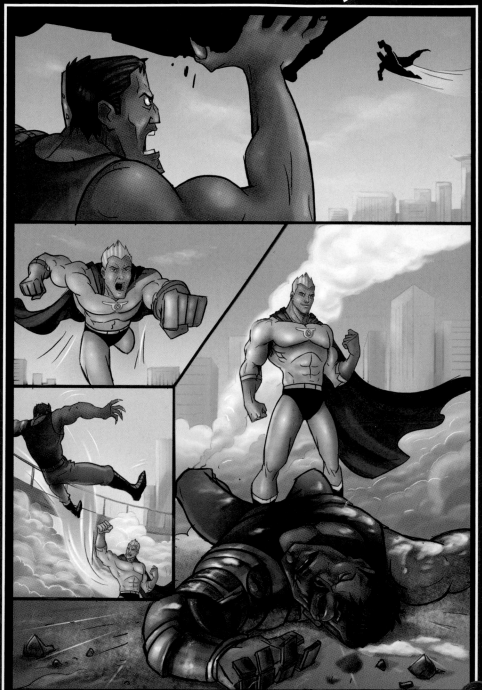

Once you're done drawing a scene, add words and sound effects. Use speech bubbles to get your characters talking. Use thought bubbles to reveal what they're thinking. Have fun with sound effects!

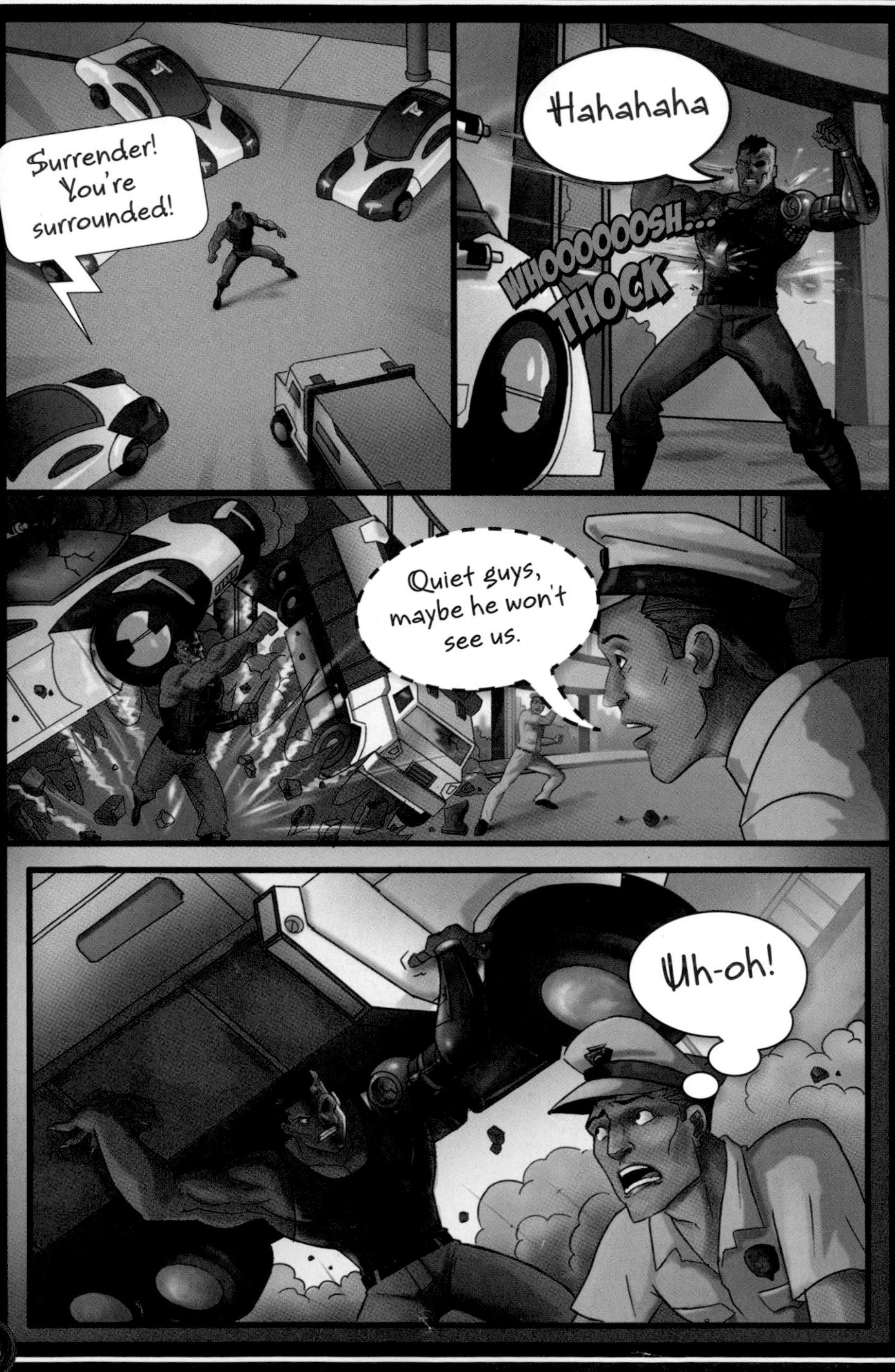

Surrender! You're surrounded!
Hahahaha
WHOOOOOOSH...
THOCK
Quiet guys, maybe he won't see us.
Uh-oh!

The style of a speech bubble can tell you if a character is talking, whispering, yelling, or thinking. Jagged lines generally stand for yelling, dotted ones for whispering, and a cloud shape is generally used to show thoughts. A speech bubble with a jagged tail indicates that the words are coming from a device like a telephone or megaphone.

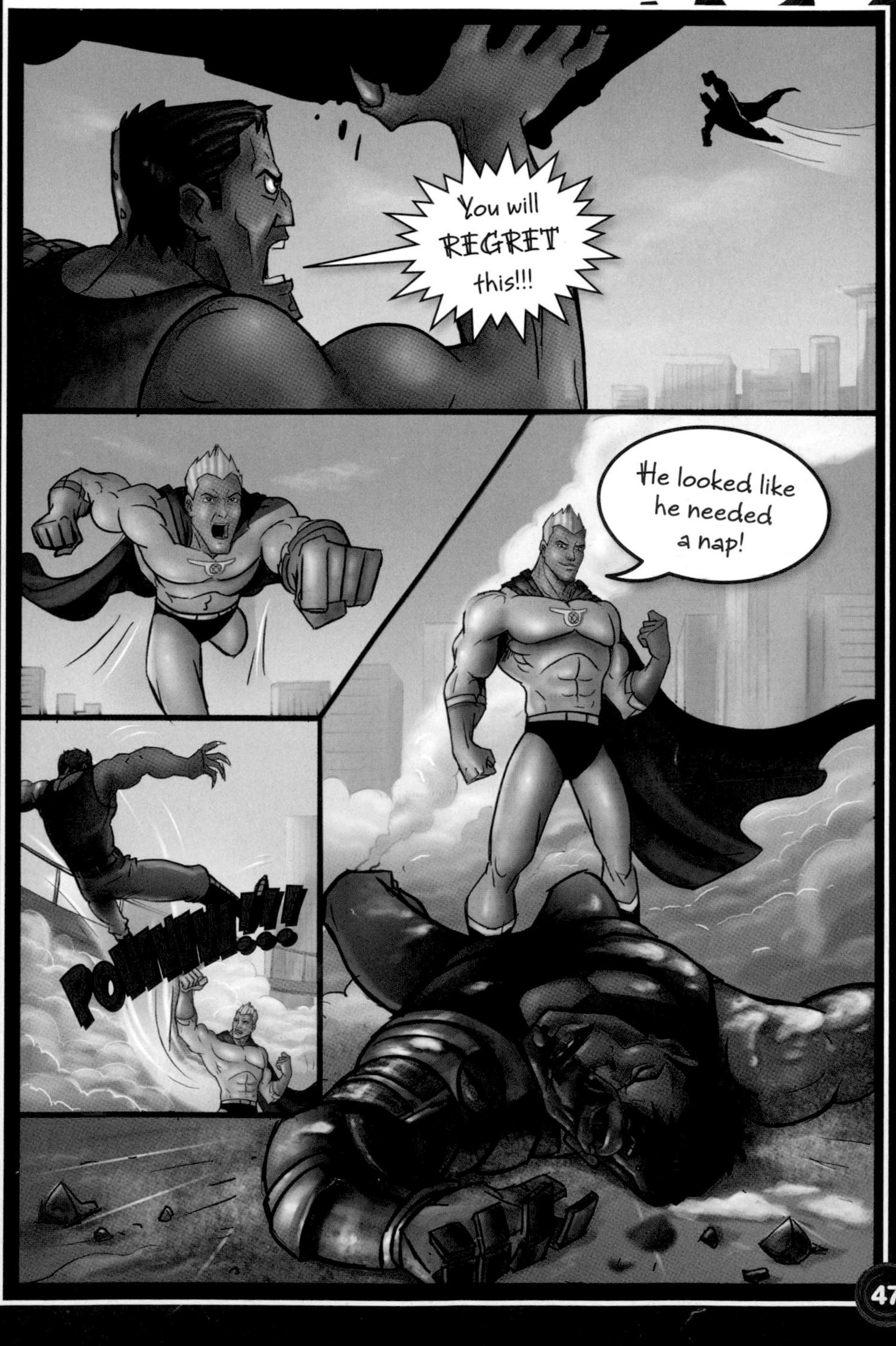
You will REGRET this!!!
He looked like he needed a nap!

READ MORE

Hanson, Anders. *Cool Drawing: The Art of Creativity for Kids!* Cool Art. Edina, Minn.: ABDO, 2009.

Sautter, Aaron. *The Boys' Guide to Drawing Aliens, Warriors, Robots and Other Cool Stuff.* Mankato, Minn.: Capstone Press, 2009.

Temple, Kathryn. *Drawing in Color.* Art for Kids. New York: Lark Books, 2009.

Thurman, Mark, and Emily Hearn. *Get Graphic! Using Storyboards to Write and Draw Picture Books, Graphic Novels, or Comic Strips.* Ontario, Canada: Pembroke Publishers Limited, 2010.

INTERNET SITES

FactHound offers a safe, fun way to find Internet sites related to this book. All of the sites on FactHound have been researched by our staff.

Here's all you do:

Visit *www.facthound.com*

Type in this code: **9781429665940**